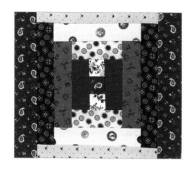

Practical Home Handbook

Patchwork

Skills & Techniques

Practical Home Handbook

Patchwork
Skills & Techniques

Dorothy Wood

LORENZ BOOKS

This edition is published by Lorenz Books

Lorenz Books is an imprint of
Anness Publishing Ltd
Hermes House, 88–89 Blackfriars Road, London
SE1 8HA
tel. 020 7401 2077; fax 020 7633 9499
www.lorenzbooks.com; info@anness.com

UK agent: The Manning Partnership Ltd, tel.
01225 478444; fax 01225 478440;
UK distributor: Grantham Book Services Ltd,
tel. 01476 541080; fax 01476 541061;

North American agent/distributor: National Book
Network, tel. 301 459 3366;
 fax 301 429 5746;

Australian agent/distributor: Pan Macmillan
Australia, tel. 1300 135 113;
fax 1300 135 103;

New Zealand agent/distributor: David Bateman
Ltd, tel. (09) 415 7664;
fax (09) 415 8892

Publisher: Joanna Lorenz
Project Editor: Simona Hill
Step by step photography: Rodney Forte
Special Photography: Nicky Dowey
Illustrator: Penny Brown
Designer: Margaret Saddler
Editorial Reader: Diane Ashmore
Production Controller: Wanda Burrows

Previously published as *Patchwork Primer* and
as part of a larger compendium, *The Practical
Encyclopedia of Sewing*

10 9 8 7 6 5 4 3 2 1

The publisher would like to thank the following
contributors whose work appears on the cover:
Jenny Parks, Kath Poxon, Rosemary Richards,
Isabel Sunderland, Jean Spencer, and Caroline
Wilkinson.

CONTENTS

INTRODUCTION

Patchwork is a traditional craft that has enjoyed a huge revival in recent years. Designing and planning your own patchwork quilt is immensely creative and satisfying. Today, straight-sided patches such as the popular Log Cabin variations can be joined, or "pieced", on a sewing machine, making a large quilt quick to complete. Most patchwork designs consist of "blocks", or units, so if a quilt is too large for a first project you can piece together a single block to make a wallhanging or cushion cover. Modern textile artists often mix patchwork with appliqué to give their work an added three-dimensional quality and create truly original works of art.

Quilting is the finishing touch for many patchwork designs, and again this can be done by hand or machine. The beautiful traditional patterns shown here include shell- and diamond-filling, and historic forms of quilting such as trapunto and Italian that were fashionable in the seventeenth and eighteenth centuries. Another lovely effect is Japanese sashiko quilting, traditionally worked in white thread on indigo-blue fabric. The simplest technique of all is tied quilting, in which the "sandwich" layers of a patchwork quilt are knotted together at regular intervals with tufts of thread.

Patchwork looks back to the world of the early American settlers and also forward to modern art. Above all, it provides the pleasure of creating something new out of small pieces, or "patches", of fabric.

Materials and equipment

Some special equipment is required for patchwork and quilting.
This list will help you to choose the correct items.

1 Air- or water-soluble pen
Marks made by these pens wash out or disappear quickly. They are useful for temporarily marking small areas.

2 Beeswax
Running thread over a piece of beeswax smooths the thread and helps prevent knots forming.

3 Craft knife and ruler
Use a metal-edged ruler when cutting templates with a craft knife. Hold the ruler with the edge facing away from the template. Score the line several times instead of trying to cut through first time.

4 Fabric
Patchwork fabric is often sold in "fat quarters" (45 x 45cm/18 x 18in), but it is usually more economical to determine the colours and quantity required and then to buy long quarters (23 x 115cm/9 x 45in) instead.

5 Freezer paper
Freezer paper (a waxed paper food wrapping) is used for accurate hand piecing and appliqué. It has a non-marking wax coating on one side that can be ironed temporarily to fabric.

6 Fusible bonding web
Fusible bonding web is a mesh of glue used to adhere pieces of appliqué to a background fabric with heat.

7 Graph paper
Use for designing patterns and making templates. Use isometric paper for triangular or diamond patterns.

8 Pins (quilting)
Long, fine, glass-headed pins are suitable for temporarily pinning layers prior to basting.

9 Pencil and sharpener
Use a sharp pencil for marking paper templates.

10 Protractor
A protractor is used to measure angles when designing patchwork and for marking notches on curved edges. Use a set of compasses to draw curved templates and some geometric shapes.

11 Quilter's quarter
Use this to add consistent 5mm/¼in seam allowances to patchwork shapes.

12 Quilting hoops/frames
These are thick and strong to hold together the multiple layers of a quilt.

13 Quilting thimble
Use a metal thimble on the middle finger of your sewing hand and a quilting thimble on the index finger of your other hand.

14 Rotary cutting set
Use with a self-healing cutting mat and ruler for speed cutting, to straighten fabric ends and to cut strips and geometric shapes.

15 Safety pins
Use special safety pins for holding quilt layers together. Quilter's safety pins have a deeper bend on one side to accommodate thick layers of wadding (batting) without crushing it.

16 Scissors
Keep separate scissors for cutting fabric and paper because paper dulls the edge of the blade. Use dress-making shears to cut fabric and sharp, pointed embroidery scissors for close work and for snipping threads.

17 Seam unpicker
Use this to cut every third stitch. Pull out the thread from the wrong side.

18 Spray glue
Spray glue is ideal for sticking paper templates to cardboard.

19 Tape measure
Useful for measuring fabric, but not for adding seam allowances.

20 Templates
Accurate templates are essential. Draw templates for hand piecing and appliqué to the finished size. Add seam allowances before cutting out the fabric. Templates for machine piecing should include the seam allowances. Quilting templates are best made from plastic or metal.

21 Template plastic
Use translucent plastic sheeting for cutting re-usable templates. Trace your design directly through the plastic, using a soft pencil.

22 Threads
For appliqué, use thread (floss) that matches the appliqué or the background or go one shade darker. Use strong quilting thread for hand quilting with beeswax, and invisible thread for machine quilting.

23 Transfer paper and pen
Draw the mirror image of a design on transfer paper and place it face down on the fabric. Rub over the design line to transfer it to the fabric.

Looking at fabric colours, tones, shades and values

Most patchwork patterns are created by the contrast between light, medium and dark fabrics. The colours or patterns you choose will affect the overall quilt design. The depth of colour is crucial to some designs such as Tumbling Blocks because light fabrics appear to come forward while dark fabrics recede. Careful placement creates an optical illusion that makes a flat block appear three-dimensional.

The depth of colour is known as the value. It's not difficult to grade one fabric from light to dark, but this value will change when you look at it against other fabrics. Fabrics appear lighter when surrounded by darker shades, and darker when surrounded by lighter shades.

Solid-colour fabrics are used to create bold contrasts in patchwork designs. You can now buy a wide range of fabrics that look solid from a distance but are actually slightly patterned. These fabrics are printed with two subtle shades of the same colour and can be used alongside solid colours to add interest.

Prints

Everyone associates printed fabrics with patchwork. Contemporary prints can be mixed with more traditional patterns for an unusual effect, or an "antique" quilt can be stitched from carefully selected prints.

Small-scale prints tend to look solid from a distance but add interest

Above: Solid colours focus the eye when used in small quantities between patterns.

and create a textured effect when viewed at close hand. Medium prints are perhaps the most popular of the print fabrics used for patchwork. Take care when placing two of these prints together in case the pattern line is blurred and the patchwork effect lost.

Large-scale prints are useful because several different colour values can be cut from the same fabric. A large-scale print generally becomes an abstract pattern when the patchwork shape is cut. Use a window template to select a particular part of the motif to enhance your patchwork design.

It is difficult to choose fabrics for a quilt from small samples. Visit your

Below: Choose patterns carefully. Large patterns in small areas do not work and small patterns look solid from a distance.

local quilt shop and take out bolts of fabric that you like and arrange them in an order that you find pleasing. By slotting in a new fabric and lifting out an old one, you will soon find a selection of fabrics that work together in terms of colour and scale. When you substitute the right fabric for one that doesn't seem right, the range of colours will appear to "lift". Be brave, try unusual combinations – you may get a pleasant surprise and a most unusual quilt into the bargain.

Using a colour wheel

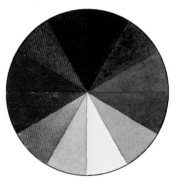

If you find it difficult to choose colours, try looking at a colour wheel. Red, yellow and blue are the three primary colours from which all others are formed. By mixing adjacent primary colours, the three secondary colours, orange, green and purple, are formed. Tertiary colours, such as blue-green, are mixed from two adjacent secondary colours.

Choose three or four adjacent colours to create a harmonious effect or go for colours opposite one another for contrast. Some of the most effective colour schemes use three adjacent colours from one side of the wheel and another from directly opposite for contrast. The primary colours create the most vibrant colour schemes but three or four tertiary colours produce a more subtle effect.

CHOOSING FABRIC

• Patchwork is often seen as a good way of using up scraps, but in fact you usually need to buy quite a lot of new fabric for a large project such as a quilt.

• The wonderful array of "fat quarters" (45 x 45cm/18 x 18in) lined up in baskets in your local needlecraft shop is very tempting but you will waste money if you buy these small pieces before you have planned your quilt and determined the actual amount required.

• Even if you only need a small quantity of one colour, it may still be better to buy a "long quarter" (23 x 115cm/ 9 x 45in) instead.

• Many quilters buy fabric made for the purpose, but it is also possible to use fabric from other sources such as clothing.

• Always use good-quality fabrics with a similar fibre content for quilt making.

• Thin or worn fabrics will not last and wadding (batting) will work through a loosely woven fabric to produce a surface haze.

• Choose closely woven fabrics, but not with so tight a weave that they will be difficult to sew.

• Visualize and plan the quilt on paper then try out a single block to make sure the colours work well together and that you like them before going on to buy large amounts of fabric.

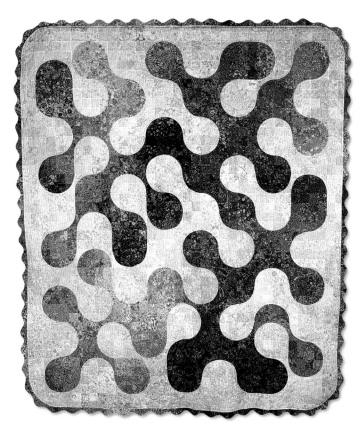

Above: Colours from the whole colour spectrum have been carefully chosen and placed to fade and merge together in this patchwork design. Over 1,500 patches have been used, all with subtle and small-scale patterns.

Preparing the fabric

Some people advocate washing and pressing the fabric before cutting, while others prefer to work with crisp new fabric and like the "antique look" achieved by the fabric shrinking slightly when the whole quilt is washed for the first time. If you choose this method ensure that all your fabrics are colourfast first.

If you want to wash them, sort the fabrics into light and dark shades and wash each pile separately in warm water with some fabric conditioner. It is not necessary to add detergent if the fabric is clean. Rinse the fabric thoroughly and hang out to dry by the selvages. Press while still slightly damp. Straighten the fabric ends and the grain before cutting.

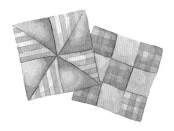

Choosing wadding (batting)

The wadding is the fabric layer that is sandwiched between the quilt top and the backing. Antique quilts were filled with anything to hand from old blankets to worn patchwork quilts. Nowadays, wadding is purpose-made in a range of fibres from polyester to wool, cotton or even silk. Patchwork suppliers stock a wide range, with each fibre type suitable for a different purpose.

Each fibre has different properties that will affect the finished look of the quilt. The finished thickness or "handle" of a quilt will depend on the type of wadding (batting) used between the layers. Polyester wadding tends to be very bouncy with a padded look, whereas cotton or wool wadding gives a flatter effect that drapes well. Most people choose polyester wadding for their first quilt but this is often rather thick, unwieldy and difficult to quilt. Buy a sample pack of wadding and try out the different types before you make your choice, by sandwiching a piece of wadding between two layers of calico or other cotton fabric. Try hand or machine stitching a small quilting design to see how easily the wadding handles.

Often it may be plain logic that makes the decision for you. If you are making a king-size quilt and want to machine quilt it, the wadding will at some stage have to be rolled up, and the roll will have to fit through the sewing machine. Once in the machine you should be able to manoeuvre it.

Types of wadding (batting)

Choose wadding (batting) carefully, because you can't change your mind after it is stitched. On some of the types of wadding mentioned here, you should leave a gap of no more than 7.5–10cm/3–4in between your quilting lines to prevent them from breaking up in the wash. On others you can leave up to 25cm/10in.

1 **50g/2oz polyester** – a thin wadding (90cm/36in wide) for quilting or padding. It is useful for making padded frames and for backing embroideries to throw the design into relief.
2 **115g/4oz polyester** – the basic wadding for quilts. It is inexpensive and fairly easy to quilt, but does not drape very well. It is sold off the roll or in quilt-sized pieces.
3 **170g/6oz polyester** – a bulky wadding that is too thick to sew and is generally used for tie quilting.
4 **Firm-needled wadding** – a 100 per cent polyester wadding, suitable for making wall hangings and bags. It holds its shape well once quilted.
5 **Polydown** – a low-loft, soft, 100 per cent resin-bonded, polyester wadding that is very easy to stitch.

6 **Thermore** – a very thin, 100 per cent polyester wadding that drapes well and is guaranteed not to "beard" (the process where strands of wadding work their way through the quilt top). It is ideal for clothing or wall quilts.
7 **Wool** – this wonderfully soft wadding is very easy to quilt and drapes beautifully. Leave no more than 7.5cm/3in between your quilting lines. A quilt made with wool wadding provides particularly good insulation but needs hand washing or dry cleaning.
8 **Cotton** – made from 80 per cent cotton, 20 per cent polyester, this wadding has slight bounce from the polyester but the cotton shrinks by up to 5 per cent, which gives an antique look to a quilt.
9 **Organic cotton** – this environmentally friendly and hypo-allergenic wadding is suitable for hand quilting. For machine quilting, use the scrim-backed version which can be quilted up to 25cm/10in apart.
10 and 11 **100 per cent cotton** – this wadding is very easy to quilt. The fibres have been needled through a strong, thin base to produce an even, stable wadding that will last for years. Available in different thicknesses, it is suitable for hand and machine quilting and the layers of stitching can be wide apart.

Getting started

Making a full-size quilt is quite a commitment of both time and money. Knowing where to begin and what design to choose can be daunting. But remember, even the most experienced quiltmaker producing amazing designs started somewhere. And the quilters of the past produced incredible work with few resources except their own creativity.

Today, we have so many gadgets all designed to improve our quilt-making that knowing what to buy and how to start to make a quilt can become a confusing experience for a novice. The following guidelines will take you through the quilt-making process one step at a time. Begin by looking at quilts in exhibitions, or ones that friends have made, to establish what kinds of designs and colour schemes appeal to you. If you are working by

hand rather than machine, accept that quilt-making is a time-consuming business and choose to work on a small-scale wall hanging or cot-size quilt first, before progressing to ambitious bed-sized quilts.

Alternately, making lots of samples of different cushion-sized blocks, then joining them all together into a quilt, is a good way to learn many of the basic techniques and which type of blocks and colours appeal to you.

With a design in mind, the next stage is to determine how big the finished piece will be. The box on the next page is a general guide to quilt sizes, but you will need to take into account whether the quilt will sit on top of the bed or touch the floor on three sides and add on an extra allowance accordingly. Draw a rectangle on graph paper to represent your quilt. Work to a reduced scale and draw a rough diagram first.

Quilt terminology

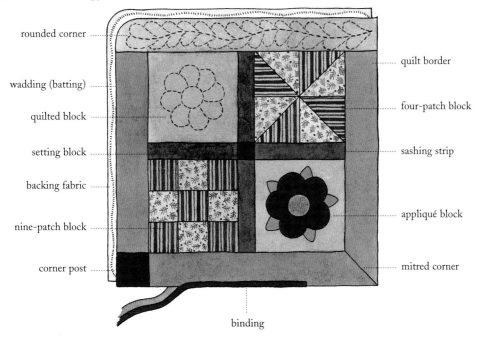

rounded corner

wadding (batting)

quilted block

setting block

backing fabric

nine-patch block

corner post

quilt border

four-patch block

sashing strip

appliqué block

mitred corner

binding

Planning a quilt design

Block quilts are easier to plan than all-over mosaic quilts (one or two patches). Whichever type you are making, it is relatively easy to determine the quantity of fabric needed for a small area and then multiply this to see what is required for a whole quilt.

Quilt composition

Although some quilts have the patchwork extending out to the edge, the majority have a border and others also have strips of fabric, called sashing, which separate the blocks. Borders and sashing alter the size and appearance of your quilt dramatically.

Plan your quilt by drawing a sketch of the blocks that will make up your quilt design on graph paper first, shading them to show the light, medium and dark fabrics. Use

photocopies for this stage if there are a lot of blocks. Try out various arrangements and look for border fabrics that will enhance the design.

When you are happy with the arrangement, draw your quilt design on graph paper. This will allow you to check the finished size and determine the fabric quantities. Size is not so crucial for a wall quilt, but the dimensions and overall design are.

Sashing and borders

Sashing and borders are cut on the lengthways grain of the fabric. Add on an extra 5cm/2in to the length of the border pieces and allow 12mm/$\frac{1}{2}$in seam allowance widthways on each strip. First determine how many strips will fit across the fabric width, then find the total number of metres or yards required.

Quilt backing

The quilt back will look best in a fabric that co-ordinates with the quilt front. Determine the total length and width of the finished quilt, then add 5–10cm/2–4in to your measurements. If the quilt back is wider than the fabric it will be necessary to join lengths together, keeping the seams equidistant from the centre.

Binding

You will also need to cut some binding strips to finish off the quilt. Standard binding strips are 5cm/2in wide. Straight binding is cut from the lengthways grain and bias binding is cut diagonally across the fabric. A 1m/1yd length of 115cm/45in wide fabric will provide about 21m/23yd of binding on the straight grain and 19m/20$\frac{1}{4}$yd cut on the bias.

Left: The blocks of this representational school houses quilt design are held together with sashing strips and setting blocks.

QUILT SIZES

Use this table as a rough guide to the size your quilt should be, but remember the measurements will vary depending on the type of patchwork and size of blocks. You will still need to measure the actual bed to establish the finished quilt size.

Baby	90–115cm/36–45in wide	x	115–137cm/45–54in long
Cot	107–122cm/42–48in wide	x	137–152cm/54–60in long
Single	142–162cm/56–64in wide	x	213–254cm/84–100in long
Double	178–203cm/70–80in wide	x	213–254cm/84–100in long
Queen	193–213cm/76–84in wide	x	228–264cm/90–104in long
King	234–254cm/92–100in wide	x	228–264cm/90–104in long
Jumbo	304–315cm/120–124in wide	x	304–315cm/120–124in long

CONVERSION CHART

You will find it easier to use the decimal equivalent for imperial measurements when working out quantities with a calculator.

Metric	Imperial	Decimal
3mm	$\frac{1}{8}$in	0.125in
5mm	$\frac{1}{4}$in	0.25in
9mm	$\frac{3}{8}$in	0.375in
1.2cm	$\frac{1}{2}$in	0.5in
1.6cm	$\frac{5}{8}$in	0.625in
1.9cm	$\frac{3}{4}$in	0.75in
2.2cm	$\frac{7}{8}$in	0.875in
2.5cm	1in	1.0in
5cm	2in	2.0in
7.5cm	3in	3.0in
10cm	4in	4.0in
13cm	5in	5.0in
15cm	6in	6.0in

CALCULATING QUANTITIES: ROAD TO HEAVEN BLOCK

CALCULATING BLOCKS AND PATCHES

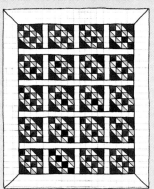

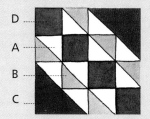

• Label each shape in the blocks with a different letter and then add up the pieces to determine how many of each shape and colour there are in the block.

For example, this block requires:

Small triangles:
10   Light fabric A
6   Medium fabric B

Large triangles:
2   Medium fabric C

Squares:
4   Dark fabric D

• Multiply the number of fabric pieces required for each shape by the number of blocks in the quilt.

• Determine how many of each shape you can cut from a fabric width, include extra for seams.

• Take off about 5cm/2in wastage across a fabric width to allow for selvages and shrinkage.

• Instead of cutting triangles, cut squares, then cut them in half across the diagonal.

• Draw a rough sketch of your quilt on graph paper, including sashing and borders. Colour or shade the design to distinguish between the different fabrics you will be using.

CALCULATING FABRIC

This example shows how to calculate the fabric required to make up a quilt in the Road to Heaven pattern made up of 20 blocks, each 30cm/12in square. Add extra for sashing and borders.

Light fabric A – Each block contains 10 triangles cut from five squares, each 9.7cm/3⅞in. For 20 blocks, you will need 100 squares. As 10 squares fit across a 115cm/45in width, you will need enough fabric for 10 rows, that is 97cm/38¾in.

Total light fabric required: 97cm/38¾in of 115cm/45in wide fabric.

Medium fabric B – Each block contains six triangles cut from three squares, each 9.7cm/3⅞in. For 20 blocks you will need 60 squares. As 10 squares fit across a 115cm/45in width, you will need enough fabric for six rows, that is 58.2cm/23¼in.

Total medium fabric required: 58.2cm/23¼in of 115cm/45in wide fabric.

Medium fabric C – Each block contains two triangles cut from one square 17.5cm/6⅞in. For 20 blocks you will need 20 squares. As six squares fit across a 115cm/45in width, you will need enough fabric for four rows, that is 70cm/27½in.

Total medium fabric required: 70cm/27½in of 115cm/45in wide fabric.

Dark fabric D – Each block contains four squares, each 9cm/3½in. For 20 blocks you will need 80 squares. As 12 squares fit across a 115cm/45in width, you will need seven rows each, that is 63cm/24½in.

Total dark fabric required: 63cm/24½in of 115cm/45in wide fabric.

Making and using templates

Different types of template are used for patchwork, quilting and appliqué. Templates for hand piecing and appliqué are cut to the exact size of the finished shape, whereas templates for machine piecing include a 5mm/¼in seam. Some patchwork templates have windows to allow the sewing and cutting lines to be drawn at the same

time. Quilting templates have windows to allow you to mark all the quilting lines.

By using a template you can reproduce an exact shape or pattern as many times as you need to. Templates must be made from a material that will stand up to repeated use, such as firm cardboard, plastic or metal.

Plastic has several advantages over cardboard: it is transparent, allowing you to trace shapes directly, and it is hard-wearing which means that templates can be re-used. If you are using cardboard, paint the edges of the template with varnish to protect them. Ready-made templates are generally made from metal or plastic.

1 Trace the shape through the plastic with a sharp, soft pencil. It may be easier to mark a dot at each corner and join them up with a ruler. Measure and mark a 5mm/¼in border all around for a machine-stitching or window template if this is required.

2 To cut out your template, use a metal-edged ruler and score along the pencil line several times. Hold the ruler very firmly to prevent it from slipping, with the edge facing away from the template. Always cut the outside line on a machine-stitching or window template.

3 To make a window template, score very carefully along the inside lines of the template. Turn the plastic around and repeat until you have cut out the middle of the template. You may have to score along each line several times to cut right through.

Marking fabric

Try to be as accurate as you can when marking fabric to make it easier for you to join the pieces accurately later. A small discrepancy in each piece can make quite a difference over a whole quilt. Use a sharp pencil on the wrong side of the fabric and keep straight edges along the fabric grain where possible.

To avoid wasting fabric, mark any borders and sashing pieces in a particular colour before cutting the patches. Mark the patchwork pieces in rows rather than dotting them about the fabric.

1 Hand-sewing, quilting and appliqué templates are cut to the exact finished size and are used to mark the stitching line only. Place the template on the fabric with the edge along the straight grain. Mark as many squares as required, leaving enough room between each shape for the two seam allowances.

2 Measure 5mm/¼in out from each edge and join the marks. A quilter's tape or a quilter's quarter tool are useful for adding the seam allowance.

The rotary cutting set

Rotary cutting is a quick and accurate way to trim fabric and cut it into simple shapes. Squares, triangles and rectangles are particularly suitable, but with practice, diamonds can be cut. You will need a rotary cutting set, a self-healing cutting mat and a special grid-marked ruler. These are an investment, but save hours of work since multiple layers can be cut without pre-marking. Reverse the instructions if you are left-handed.

1 Fold the fabric in half, matching selvages. Steam press the layers. Fold in half again and press. Place the folded fabric on the mat. Align a crossways marking on the ruler with a fold. Roll the blade of the rotary cutter up and down the ruler edge.

2 Turn the fabric around so that the cut edge is to the left. Use the markings on the ruler to cut the width of strip you require plus 12mm/ ¹⁄₂in extra for seam allowances. Cut as many strips as required. Remember that each strip has four layers.

3 Turn the first strip around and align a crossways marking on the ruler with the bottom edge. Trim off 9mm/³⁄₈in at one end. Cut the strip into squares. Each square should be the same as the finished size plus 12mm/¹⁄₂in seam allowance.

4 To cut triangles from squares, add 2.2cm/⁷⁄₈in to the size of the finished triangle, measured down a straight side, and cut the square that size. Cut in half diagonally to make the triangles. For quarter-square triangles, cut the square 3cm/1¹⁄₄in larger than the finished triangle and cut diagonally across in both directions.

5 To cut a short diamond, cut strips the width of the diamond plus 12mm/ ¹⁄₂in for seams. Align the edge of the strip with the 60° line on the ruler and trim off the end. Keeping the 60° line along the edge of the strip, cut the diamonds the same width as the strips using the grid lines on the ruler or the mat as a guide.

6 Cut a long diamond in the same way, lining the edge of the strip with the 45° line on the ruler.

USING SCISSORS

• Always cut fabrics with a sharp blade, cutting exactly along the pencil line.

• Scissors are useful for intricate shapes and curves.

• Keep the fabric as close to the table as possible. Cut with long strokes along the main lines before cutting into separate shapes. For better accuracy, cut single layers.

Making mosaic quilts

When fabric was a precious commodity and people were reluctant to waste even the smallest scrap, fabric from old clothes and furnishings was set aside until there were sufficient pieces to join together to make a patchwork quilt.

One- and two-patch quilts

Originally the patchwork cloth was lined with thin wool blankets to make bedcovers. The patches were originally sewn together in a random fashion or in strips, but as fabric became more available, geometric shapes and intricate patterns were devised by quilt-makers to show off their skills and expertise.

Mosaic quilts were one of the most popular early patchwork quilt designs. These are made up from one or two shapes pieced together to create an

all-over pattern and are known as one- or two-patch quilts. These quilts were usually made from hexagons and diamonds and hand pieced over paper templates. Grandmother's Flower Garden is probably the best-known example of this traditional type of hand-sewn patchwork. Sometimes the papers were left in the patchwork and this can help to accurately date an old quilt.

Tumbling Blocks and Trip Around the World are two examples of modern one-patch mosaic quilts.

one-patch block

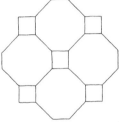
two-patch block

Below: This Tumbling Blocks design is a mosaic quilt made from thousands of tiny silk diamonds. Try looking at it from different directions to see the effect of the optical illusion.

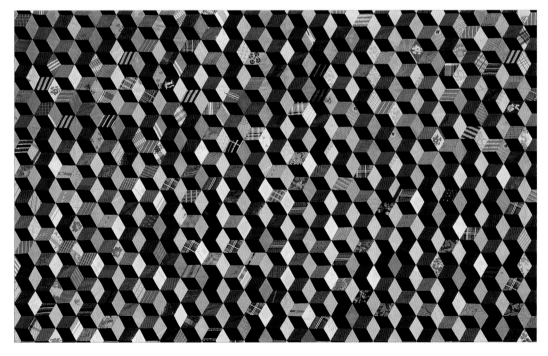

Hand-piecing a one-patch block without papers

Tumbling Blocks is a popular one-patch pattern that uses three short diamonds, that are all the same size, sewn together at different angles to make a hexagon. By using different shades of fabric in each block, a fascinating optical illusion is created. Each diamond in the hexagon is a light, medium or dark fabric.

In this simplest form of Tumbling Blocks patchwork all the hexagons are identical in size – it is the way they are put together which affects the overall appearance. The dark fabric can appear to be on the left, right or on top of the blocks, depending on which way the patchwork is viewed. You can make a more complicated pattern by using different colours and keeping the light, medium and dark fabrics in the same position as you sew the hexagons together.

1 Use a window template to draw the diamond shape on the wrong side of the fabric, keeping two opposite sides parallel to the straight grain of the fabric. Make sure the seam allowance is clearly marked on the fabric. Cut the pieces out carefully along the outside lines. Add a 5mm/ ¼in seam allowance if using an ordinary template.

2 Pin two different patches with right sides together. Make sure that the pencil-mark corners match exactly by pushing a pin through from one side to the other. Begin with a couple of back stitches and sew small running stitches along the pencil line. Stop at the first corner and work another two back stitches to secure the thread.

3 Fold the third diamond in half and insert it between the two layers. Pin the seam on two sides to complete the hexagon. Pin the point where the three pieces come together and secure this with a back stitch.

4 Sew across the two sides, making sure you keep to the marked line. Finish off with a couple of tiny back stitches.

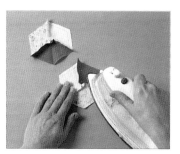

5 Press the seams to one side in the same direction so that the seams swirl open in the centre. Make six hexagons for each tower block.

6 Arrange the hexagons with the dark diamond in the same position on each one. Sew the hexagons together matching the inset points carefully. Press the seams to one side.

Hand-piecing a one-patch block with papers

Grandmother's Flower Garden takes its name from the way hexagons are arranged to create the effect of flower borders surrounded by a garden path. The "path" around the outside edge is traditionally cream to represent stone, or green for grass. Although it is a simple single-patch quilt, there are a multitude of different ways to arrange the patches and colours. In this arrangement two dark fabrics (blue and deep pink), one medium (the cream floral), and one light fabric (the cream path) are used.

The easiest way to stitch hexagons is by piecing them over paper templates. Cut the papers to the exact finished size and baste the fabric in place. You can use freezer paper to achieve very crisp edges.

1 Cut a hexagonal template and use it to draw and cut out 37 hexagonal paper shapes. Use thick paper so that the fabric can be folded over it accurately.

2 Draw the hexagon on the wrong side of the fabric, adding a 5mm/¼in seam allowance around each one. Cut the required number of patches from each colour.

3 Pin a paper shape in the centre of the wrong side of each fabric hexagon. Fold over one edge of the seam allowance at a time and baste in place. Take a small basting stitch across each corner to hold the overlapping folds flat. It is best to begin with a knot and finish with a back stitch to make the basting threads easy to remove.

4 Hold two patchwork shapes with right sides together and the corners matching to join them along the required edge. Start with two tiny back stitches into the seam allowance, then oversew the edges together. Use a fine needle to keep the stitches very small. Make sure the needle is straight when going through the fabric so that the two shapes will open out flat.

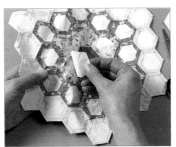

5 Build up the design, working outwards in rings. Once complete, take out the basting threads by undoing the back stitches and pulling the knot gently. Lift out the papers carefully in case they are caught in the stitching. Press the patchwork on the wrong side and on the front with a pressing cloth. The garden motif can be appliquéd on to a cushion cover or joined to other motifs to make a quilt.

Above: This simple one-patch quilt has been machine quilted and small buttons added for decoration.

Left: The traditional Grandmother's Flower Garden is stitched entirely by hand.

Below left: A drawing from a Roman pavement was the basis for this two-patch quilt, made using the same method of working over paper. Squares and elongated hexagons have been used.

Below: A diamond and a square form the basis of this lively two-patch design.

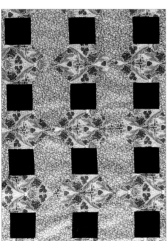

Joining patchwork by machine

Machine stitching is a quick and accurate way to join patchwork. As the seam allowances are included on templates for machine piecing, they do not need to be marked on the fabric. Instead, use the side of the presser foot as a guide for sewing a 5mm/¼in seam.

It is a good idea to test your machine first by positioning the fabric exactly on the edge of the presser foot and stitching a test piece in order to measure the seam allowance. It may be easier to adjust the needle position than to guide the fabric further in or out. A slight discrepancy won't be noticeable when stitching strips or squares, but will be obvious when you come to match triangles or diamonds to a square.

If the fabric was steam-pressed and cut with a rotary cutter, pins should not be necessary, although beginners may feel happier using them. Use pins when matching different-shaped pieces, curved edges and patchwork seams.

Sewing squares together

Place the two pieces with right sides together and position under the presser foot. Turn the hand wheel to take the needle into the fabric a seam allowance' width from the raw edges and then machine stitch the seam, stopping a seam allowance' width from the raw edge of the fabric.

Chain piecing

Patchwork pieces can be chain stitched. Stitch to the end of a patch and bring the needle out of the fabric to its highest point. Raise the presser foot and place the next patch under the foot. Continue, leaving small gaps between patches, then cut apart and press.

Sewing diamonds

It is advisable to secure the edges of seams that will be set in with others by reverse stitching at each end of the seam. Mark the point where the seam allowances will meet with a dot before sewing. Join shapes with slanting sides, such as triangles and diamonds, with the corners offset by 5mm /¹/₄in so that the edges align perfectly when pressed flat.

Sewing right-angle triangles

1   A large patchwork block is made from small shapes that are sewn together. Determine the stitching order before you start, such as sewing triangles together to make squares first. Press the seam to one side and trim the points off the seam allowance as shown.

2   Use pins to hold seamed patchwork pieces together while sewing. Try to sew across the pressed seam to ensure the presser foot runs smoothly over the top. Stitch slowly over the pins to prevent the needle hitting one and breaking.

Pressing seams

While pressing is never a favourite part of making up a patchwork quilt, it is essential. The iron and ironing board should be constantly set up while you are sewing and every single patch should be pressed as it is sewn to another. Miss this step and you may well have uneven seams.

Finger pressing

Small pieces of patchwork can be opened out and creased temporarily with the side of your thumb. Work from the right side of the fabric, keeping both seam allowances to one side. Only ever do this with squares or rectangles. Press curved seams with an iron.

Pressing straight seams

Always press patchwork seam allowances to one side. This makes the seam stronger and prevents it from bursting open. Press the seams towards the dark side if possible or away from an area to be quilted. Use a pressing cloth to prevent unwelcome glazing when pressing from the right side.

Pressing curves

To press fabric, lift the iron up and place it down again, rather than moving it over the fabric. Use a steam iron or a damp pressing cloth. Press curved seams so that the seam allowances lie flat. If this seam had been pressed the other way, the excess patterned fabric would have formed folds on the underside.

Pressing multi-seams

1 When pressing multi-seam joins in hand-pieced patchwork, swirl the seam allowances to open them out and reduce bulk. Press on the wrong side and again from the right side with a pressing cloth.

2 Press seams in the opposite direction where they join to reduce bulk. Press the whole block from the wrong side. In this block all the seam allowances have been pressed away from the light fabric where possible and the seams pressed in opposite directions where two seams meet.

3 No matter how carefully you piece the patchwork, there will always be one or two puckers where seams join. Blocks made from cotton fabrics can be steam-pressed from the right side to smooth out the wrinkles before proceeding to quilt.

Speed-piecing a one-patch block

The square is the simplest shape to sew. Trip Around the World, also known as Sunshine and Shadow, is a simple block made from squares. The pattern is formed by careful arrangement of light, medium and dark fabrics. Depending on where you place the dark squares, you can produce a chequerboard effect or diamonds in bands of light and shade which create a sunshine and shadow effect.

Trip Around the World

Draw out and colour in different patterns on graph paper in light, medium and dark shades. Use the designs below as a guide. Once you have decided on the arrangement, determine how many squares you require in each colour to complete a row the required length. Add up the number of squares in each colour for the complete quilt. Allow extra fabric for seams and for the sashing, borders and binding. When working on a large scale, arrange the blocks on a flat surface before stitching.

Below: Just a few of the different combinations for this design are show here.

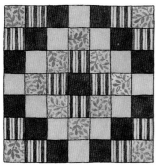

1 Place the different fabrics one on top of the other and steam press the layers together. Lift the fabric on to a cutting mat. Trim the edge and then cut strips of the required width allowing 12mm/¹/₂in for seam allowances. Turn the strips around and cut into squares.

2 Arrange the squares into the block pattern. Take the first two squares from the top row and sew together. Chain sew the first two squares from each row to save time.

3 Press the seam of the first two squares to one side. Continue adding a square at a time until the top row is complete. Sew the other rows together in the same way. Press the seam allowances in adjacent rows in opposite directions.

4 Pin the first two rows together at each join making sure the seams are aligned exactly. If the seams have been pressed correctly they should lie in opposite directions. Stitch the remaining rows to complete the block. Press all these seams in the same direction. Press all the row seams in the same direction. This creates a strong join.

Above: The squares in the Trip Around the World block can be cut small to make a series of blocks that can be set together with sashing strips or larger to make a whole quilt finished off with wide borders in the Amish style.

Above: The blocks of this quilt have been arranged in the Amish style. Pennsylvanian Amish community quilts have one overall design rather than a block construction and are made by working from the centre out towards the edges. This design has the characteristic wide borders typical of Amish quilts but the shape and fabrics are not authentic. The Amish quilts were usually a square shape made of solid colour fabrics as patterned material was considered too worldly. The Amish preferred dark, sombre plain fabrics that reflected their simple way of life.

Working with right-angle triangles

Many patchwork patterns are created from two or four right-angle (or half-square) triangles stitched into squares. Hopscotch, Magic Triangles, and Port and Starboard, for example, are all one-patch designs made up entirely from right-angle triangles. These can be machine stitched and chain pieced or worked by hand in the traditional way.

To make a 30cm/12in block, use 9.7cm/3⅞in squares cut in half. It is important when cutting and sewing triangles to create perfect points. The best way to achieve this is by using crisp fabric, cutting accurately and then sewing exactly 5mm/¼in from the edge or marked line. If the fabric is flimsy, spray it lightly with starch and press it before cutting.

For half-square triangles (made up of two different coloured triangles), cut two squares 2.2cm/⅞in larger than the size of the finished block. For quarter-square triangles (made up of four triangles, usually with at least two colours), cut two squares 3cm/1¼in larger than the finished block.

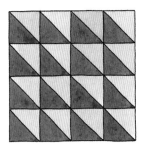

Hopscotch

Margaret's Choice

Electric Fan

Magic Triangles

Port and Starboard

Dutchman's Puzzle

Half-square triangles

Steam press two contrasting colour squares right sides together. Draw a diagonal line joining two corners on the wrong side of the lighter fabric. Stitch 5mm/¼in to each side of the drawn line. Cut along the drawn line.

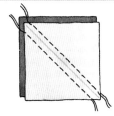

Above: Just two simple blocks make up this stunning quilt design. A plain black block is surrounded by ten pink and black half-square triangles. The blocks are joined together and set on-point to represent fish. The design looks deceptively difficult, but is infact a good example of how simply constructed patches can be arranged to appear complex.

Quarter-square triangles

Make two half-square triangles from contrasting colours. Place right sides together, alternating the colours. Press the pieces together. Draw a diagonal line joining opposite corners. Stitch and cut as before.

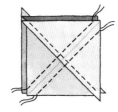

Speed-cutting and sewing half-square triangles

If you want to cut down on the amount of drawing around templates and chain piecing, use this method of speed-cutting and sewing half-square triangles. Make each square 2.2cm/⁷⁄₈in larger than the finished triangle. Mark the squares on the wrong side of the lightest coloured fabric and draw a diagonal through each square. You can also buy a special template for marking the stitching lines, which will make this part easier. Take care over cutting and sewing rows of triangles and you should get perfect points each time.

Above: Speed-piecing saves hours of laborious cutting.

1 With right sides together, place the lightest colour fabric on top of the darker one. Match the grain lines and steam press. This seals the layers together and makes cutting easier.

2 Place the template on top and mark through the slots on the grid. Alternatively, draw the grid and then mark a diagonal line through two corners. Stitch 5mm/¹⁄₄in to each side of the diagonal line.

3 Machine stitch along the marked diagonal lines, extending the stitching beyond all marked lines. For every square drawn, you will get two pieced patchwork squares.

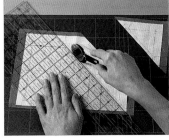

4 Place the stitched fabric on a cutting mat. Cut along the middle of the stitching lines and then along the square grid lines to make half-square triangles. Press the seam allowances to the dark side.

5 Pin and stitch two half-square triangles together. Press the seam towards the dark side. The pieced squares can be chain stitched together, but make sure you leave a long enough chain between the patches to cut them apart easily.

6 When half-square triangles are sewn together in strips, the points do not go right to the edge. This is known as a "hung point". Make each point exactly 5mm/¹⁄₄in from the raw edge and you should get a row of perfect points when stitched.

7 Pin the rows of triangles together, matching the seams and raw edges carefully. Machine stitch 5mm/¹⁄₄in from the edge. Where possible, press the seam away from the light fabric.

American block quilts

The European settlers took patchwork to America, but over the years a distinctive American tradition emerged. In the nineteenth century, quilts were made to commemorate special events. Some of the earliest patterns were in the form of stars created to celebrate the founding of a new state, such as the Ohio Star. These stars were pieced together from simple shapes into square blocks, which were sewn together with sashing strips.

Block-style patchwork became the mainstay of American quilt-making. Patchwork shapes were pieced together to form patterns and given names depending on what the pattern resembled. The names varied depending on where the quilt was made, but often it reflected the lives and surroundings of the people who created the pattern. Frequently the same block design can be known by many evocative names.

Block quilts are designed on a grid of squares. The most common designs are based on four or nine patches making up the block. Many quilts also depend on blocks being joined together to form an overall pattern.

Types of block quilt

Four patch
A four-patch block can be divided into four equal squares. Each individual patch does not necessarily contain the same pattern, but on some, such as the Windmill block, the same patch is rotated to form the pattern. The four-patch block is quite simple to make as the individual pieces tend to be quite large, and easy to sew together. It is a good first block to try.

Nine patch
A nine-patch block is created on a three-by-three square grid. A variety of simple patterns can be created from just one or two shapes, with the most simple being nine squares joined together. The complex nine-patch design illustrated is known as Puss in the Corner. It is created from different size triangles and a square.

Five patch
The five-patch block is less common. It is designed on a five-by-five grid. The pieces are not necessarily all small as some shapes run over two or three squares of the grid. Here the large triangles at the corner of the centre patch could be cut as large triangles or as a square and two smaller triangles. Determine a stitching order before beginning to piece more complex blocks.

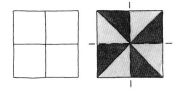

Seven patch
Seven-patch blocks are drawn out on a seven-by-seven grid. The most popular seven-patch block is a pattern called Bear's Paw, also known as Hands All Around or Duck's Foot in the Mud. The block resembles four paws facing out from the centre. It is effective when made up in two contrasting plain fabrics. Cut the shapes as large as possible, using strips rather than squares between the paws.

Four-patch blocks

Traditional patchwork blocks are still one of the most popular methods used to piece together a quilt. The same block can be repeated over the whole quilt or different blocks can be made in co-ordinating colours and joined together with sashing strips. Today we have much less time for quilt-making and look for ways of speeding up the process. There are many books on the market containing templates for different block patterns, but it is much quicker and more accurate to cut the patchwork shapes with a rotary cutter. Below you will find cutting plans for making 30cm/12in square four-patch blocks in many popular patterns, along with a suggested diagramatic stitching plan. Although the different sizes may seem awkward at first, you will soon become familiar with some of the measurements.

Cutting plans will work for traditional hand or machine sewing. Once you have cut all the pieces, analyse the block to establish the best stitching order. It is a good idea to sew straight sides together where possible and avoid having to set in pieces. As a rough guide, sew triangles together to form squares, then sew the squares into rows before sewing the rows into blocks. If you intend to speed piece any of these designs, select your fabric carefully. Speed-piecing methods work well on plain or small patterned fabrics that do not have a definite direction. Directional patterns may turn out the wrong way in the block.

Double Pinwheel

Cutting

1 From cream, cut one square 18.4cm/7¼in. Cut across the diagonals into four triangles (A).

2 From blue, cut one square 18.4cm/7¼in. Cut into four triangles (B).

3 From patterned fabric, cut two squares, each 17.5cm/6⅞in. Cut each into two triangles (C).

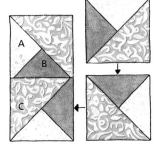

1 Cut all the pieces required for the block. Pin the small triangles together along one short side and machine stitch 5mm/¼in from the edge. Press the seam towards the darker coloured triangle.

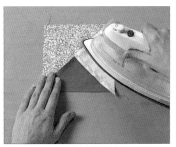

2 Pin the long edge of the large triangle to the pieced triangle. Machine stitch and press the seam away from the lightest fabric. Trim any points that are jutting out from the square.

3 Arrange the squares in the pinwheel pattern. Pin and sew the two left-hand squares together, then join the other two. Press the seams in opposite directions then pin and stitch both rectangles together to complete the block.

Windmill

Cutting

1 From cream, cut two squares, each 17.5cm/6⅞in. Cut each across the diagonal into two triangles (A).

2 From blue, cut two squares, each 17.5cm/6⅞in. Cut each across the diagonal into two triangles (B).

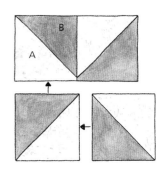

Road to Heaven

Cutting

1 From cream, cut five squares, each 10cm/3⅞in. Cut each into two triangles (A).

2 From blue, cut one square 17.5cm/6⅞in. Cut into two triangles (B).
• Cut three squares, each 10cm/3⅞in. Cut each into two triangles (C).

3 From navy, cut four squares, each 7.5cm/3in (D).

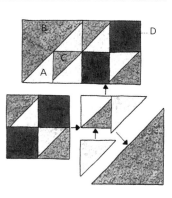

Flower Basket

Cutting

1 From cream, cut one square 17.5cm/6⅞in. Cut into two triangles (A). Discard one triangle.
• Cut two rectangles, each 9 x 16.5cm/3½ x 6½in (B).
• Cut eight squares, each 10cm/3⅞in. Cut each into two triangles (C).

2 From blue, cut three squares, each 10cm/3⅞in. Cut each into two triangles (D).

3 From navy, cut one square 17.5cm/6⅞in. Cut into two triangles (E). Discard one triangle.
• Cut one square 10cm/3⅞in. Cut into two triangles (F).

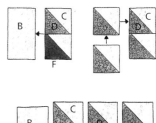

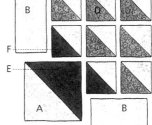

Flock of Geese

Cutting

1 From pink, cut one square 17.5cm/6⅞in. Cut into two triangles (A).
• Cut four squares, each 10cm/3⅞in. Cut each into two triangles (B).

2 From patterned fabric, cut one square 17.5cm/6⅞in. Cut into two triangles (C).
• Cut four squares, each 10cm/3⅞in. Cut each into two triangles (D).

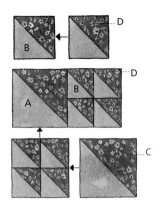

Crockett Cabin

Cutting

1 From cream, cut two squares, each 10cm/3⅞in. Cut each into two triangles (A).
• Cut eight squares, each 8.9cm/3½in (B).

2 From pink, cut two squares, each 10cm/3⅞in. Cut each into two triangles (C).
• Cut four squares, each 8.9cm/3½in (D).

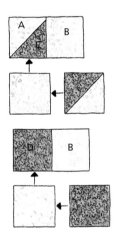

Crosses and Losses

Cutting

1 From green, cut one square 17.5cm/6⅞in. Cut across the diagonal into two triangles (A).
• Cut two squares, each 10cm/3⅞in. Cut each into two triangles (B).
• Cut four squares, each 8.9cm/3½in (C).

2 From patterned fabric, cut one square 17.5cm/6⅞in. Cut across the diagonal into two triangles (D)
• Cut two squares, each 10cm/3⅞in. Cut each into two triangles (E).

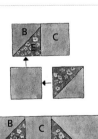

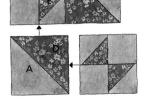

Spool and Bobbin

Cutting

1 From cream, cut two squares, each 16.5cm/6½in (A).
• Cut two squares, each 10cm/3⅞in. Cut each across the diagonal into two triangles (B).

2 From pink, cut one square 17.5cm/6⅞in. Cut across the diagonal into two triangles (C).
• Cut two squares, each 8.9cm/3½in (D).

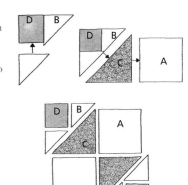

Right: Panels in this "sampler" quilt feature the following nine designs: 1, 3, 13 and 15 Bear's Paw; 2 Honey Bee; 4 and 11 Churn Dash; 5 Dutchman's Puzzle; 6 and 10 Patience Corner; 7 and 12 Star of Hope; 8 Le Moyne Star; and 9 Jenny's Star.

The design features four-, seven- and nine-patch sample blocks. Though the blocks appear random, they have been arranged so that colours and corners are symmetrical. The sashing strips are made of three strips pieced together, and the corner posts are all small nine-patch blocks.

Making a "sampler" quilt is a good way of trying out lots of new designs. Keep the colour scheme co-ordinated and the finished blocks a uniform size.

1	2	3
4	5	6
7	8	9
10	11	12
13	14	15

Nine-patch blocks

If you enjoy working with small units, working with nine-patch blocks is a good way to learn to accurately match seams. Many of the designs shown here could be further divided to make the piecing sequence challenging.

Contrary Wife

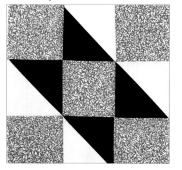

Cutting

1 From cream, cut two squares, each 12.4cm/4⁷⁄₈in. Cut each into two triangles (A).

2 From blue, cut five squares, each 11.4cm/4¹⁄₂in (B).

3 From navy, cut two squares, each 12.4cm/4⁷⁄₈in. Cut each into two triangles (C).

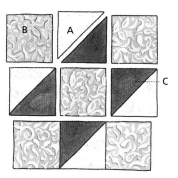

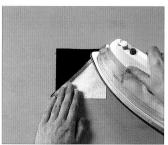

1 Pin the triangles together along the longer edge and machine stitch 5mm/¹⁄₄in from the edge. Press the seam towards the dark coloured triangle. Trim any points that jut out from the square.

2 For the top and bottom rows, pin a blue patch on to each side of the pieced square. Machine stitch 5mm/¹⁄₄in from the edge and press the seam away from the lighest colour.

3 For the middle row, pin and sew a pieced square to each side of a plain square, making sure that the pieced squares all face in the right direction when opened out. Join the rows together and press the seams to one side.

Churn Dash

Cutting

1 From cream, cut two squares, each 12.4cm/4⁷⁄₈in. Cut each into two triangles (A).
• Cut one square 11.4cm/4¹⁄₂in (B).
• Cut four rectangles, each 6.4 x 11.4cm/2¹⁄₂ x 4¹⁄₂in (C).

2 From blue, cut two squares, each 12.4cm/4⁷⁄₈in. Cut each into two triangles (D).
• Cut four rectangles, each 6.4 x 11.4cm/2¹⁄₂ x 4¹⁄₂in (E).

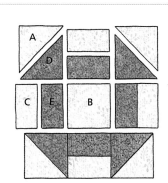

Jacob's Ladder

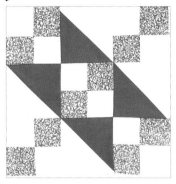

Cutting

1 From cream, cut two squares, each 12.4cm/4⅞in. Cut each into two triangles (A).
• Cut ten squares, each 6.4cm/2½in (B).

2 From blue pattern, cut ten squares, each 6.4cm/2½in (C).

3 From solid blue, cut two squares, each 12.4cm/4⅞in. Cut each into two triangles (D).

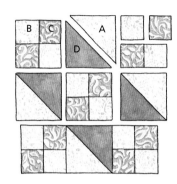

Puss in the Corner

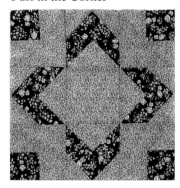

Cutting

1 From pink, cut one square 13.3cm/5¼in. Cut into four triangles (A).
• Cut two squares, each 12.4cm/4⅞in. Cut each into two triangles (B).
• Cut one square 11.4cm/4½in for the centre (C).
• Cut eight squares, each 7.3cm/2⅞in. Cut each into two triangles (D).

2 From dark fabric, cut one square 13.3cm/5¼in. Cut into four triangles (E).
• Cut four squares, each 7.3cm/2⅞in. Cut each into two triangles (F).
• Cut four squares, each 6.4cm/2½in for the corners (G).

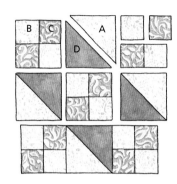

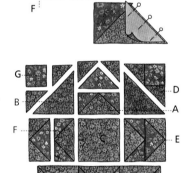

Darting Birds

Cutting

1 From cream pattern, cut three squares, each 12.4cm/4⅞in. Cut each into two triangles (A).
• Cut one square 11.4cm/4½in (B).

2 From pink, cut two squares, each 12.4cm/4⅞in. Cut each into two triangles (C).

3 From green, cut one square 12.4cm/4⅞in. Cut into two triangles (D).
• Cut two squares, each 11.4cm/4½in (E).

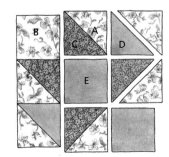

Steps to the Altar

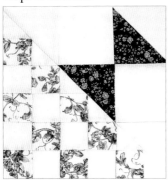

Cutting

1 From cream, cut six squares, each 6.4cm/2½in (A).
• Cut three squares, each 7.3cm/2⅞in. Cut each into two triangles (B).
• Cut two squares, each 11.4cm/4½in (C).
• Cut two squares, each 12.4cm/4⅞in. Cut each into two triangles (D). Discard one D triangle.

2 From pink pattern, cut nine squares, each 6.4cm/2½in (E).

3 From dark pattern fabric, cut one square 12.4cm/4⅞in. Cut across the diagonal into two triangles (F).

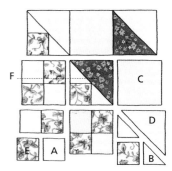

Eccentric Star

Cutting

1 From cream pattern, cut four squares, each 12.4cm/4⅞in. Cut each into two triangles (A).

2 From pink pattern, cut one 11.4cm/4½in square for the centre.

3 From red, cut four squares, each 12.4cm/4⅞in. Cut each into two triangles (C).

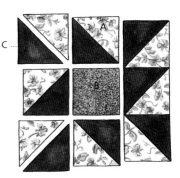

Shoo Fly

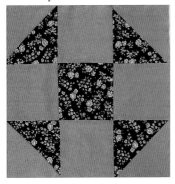

Cutting

1 From pink, cut two squares, each 12.4cm/4⅞in. Cut each into two triangles (A).
• Cut four squares, each 11.4cm/4½in (B).

2 From dark pattern fabric, cut two squares, each 12.4cm/4⅞in. Cut each into two triangles (C).
• Cut one square 11.4cm/4½in (D).

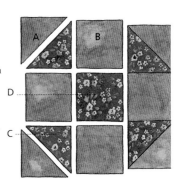

Cat's Cradle

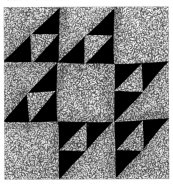

Cutting

1 From blue pattern fabric, cut three squares, each 12.4cm/4⁷/₈in (A).
• Cut three squares, each 11.4cm/4¹/₂in. Cut each in half across the diagonal (B).
• Cut three squares, each 7.3cm/2⁷/₈in. Cut each in half across the diagonal (C).

2 From navy, cut nine squares, each 7.3cm/2⁷/₈in. Cut each in half across the diagonal (D).

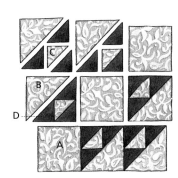

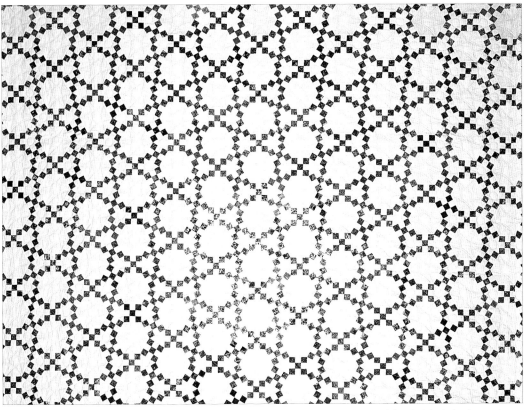

Above: This exquisite geometric design has been entirely hand stitched. The nine-patch blocks are made of 2.5cm/1in squares of cream and small floral prints. Hexagons and triangles form the remainder of the design. When viewed from a distance this mosaic-like composition appears to be formed of interlocking circles.

Piecing star designs

One of the most popular patchwork motifs, the star has been used throughout history as a divine symbol in the decorative arts of all civilizations. The simplified star appears in hundreds of different forms throughout the world with varying numbers of points.

The star was a very popular motif in colonial America. Some patchwork star motifs were designed to commemorate the creation of a state, such as the Ohio Star or the Virginia Star, and others like the Le Moyne Star were named after famous people.

Patchwork stars normally have six, eight or 12 points and are generally made from triangles or diamonds. The easiest stars to make are based on a block pattern. The Ohio Star is a nine-patch design as is the more unusual 54/40 or Fight Star. Other stars, such as the Le Moyne Star, are created from diamonds using an eight-seam join.

Right: Echoing and interlocking stars pieced in vibrant and muted colour silks make up this Star of India design.

54/40 or Fight Star

Women weren't supposed to have political opinions in the nineteenth century but often used their quilt making to express their views. The 54/40 or Fight Star was created in response to the dispute between the British Hudson Bay Company and the United States of America over the northern boundary of the United States in 1818. The numbers refer to the degree of latitude that the Americans wanted to establish as the boundary between Canada and the USA. After a bitter dispute a treaty was signed in 1846 which established the boundary where it is today.

1 Using the template provided, trace the patchwork pieces on to template plastic and cut them out. Calculate the number of pieces required and draw them on to the different fabrics. Mark 5mm/¼in seam allowances around each piece and cut out.

2 Put the middle-sized corner of a dark triangle and the point of the light triangle together. Use a pin or the needle to match the corners of the seam allowances exactly. Sew the pieces together along the marked line on the long edge with tiny running stitches. Join the second dark triangle to the other side.

Right: Half- and quarter-square triangles and single patches made into different-sized star blocks form the basis of this design. The collage-like design is an exercise in using a restricted colour palette of cleverly placed blues, greys and pinks.

3 Press the seam allowances towards the dark side, then join four small squares together to form five blocks. Press the centres open, spiralling the seam allowances to reduce bulk. Pin and stitch the pieced squares together in rows in the correct order. Press the seams to one side, then press seams in adjacent rows to the opposite side.

4 Pin the rows together, matching the seams carefully. Stitch the rows together and press all the seams to one side.

Above: The Fight Star, a nine-patch block, looks complicated to piece, but five of the nine blocks are made of a simple four-patch design in which small single patches are joined together.

Le Moyne Star

The Le Moyne Star is made from eight diamonds that meet in the centre in an eight-seam join. This representational design takes practice to master and accurate cutting and piecing are essential.

The star can be made by hand or by machine. The centre of a hand stitched, eight-seam join is pressed in a spiral to reduce bulk. The finished star can then be made into a block by insetting squares into the corners and triangles along each side.

 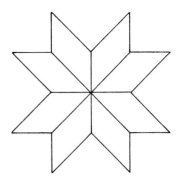

1 Using the template cut eight diamonds and mark a dot in the corners of the seam allowances on the wrong side. Pin and stitch pairs of diamonds together between the dots, reverse stitching at each end to secure the threads. Press the seams to one side. Pin two pairs of diamonds together matching seam allowances.

2 Place the pieces under the presser foot. Turn the hand wheel to make sure the needle goes in exactly at the point of the seam allowance. Sew the seam and press to one side. Pin the two halves of the star together. Check that the centre point matches by inserting a pin through all the layers. Stitch slowly over the pin.

3 When the star is machine-pieced, press the final seams to one side. If the star has been hand-pieced, spiral the seam allowances and open out the centre. Press the seams to one side and then press the centre rosette flat.

VIRGINIA STAR

The Virginia Star is a complicated block made from a large number of diamonds.

• Although the star can be stitched by machine, it is probably safer to sew it by hand, as diamonds may need careful adjustment to get the points absolutely accurate.

• Use the template provided.

Setting in patchwork pieces

When used to fill in angles such as the spaces between the points of a Le Moyne Star, patchwork pieces have to be "set in". Pieces can be set in by hand or by machine, but take care that the seams on the star are stitched accurately along the seam allowances and stop 5mm/¹⁄₄in from the edge. Secure the ends of the eight-point seam by tying off the threads or with a few back stitches.

1 With right sides together, pin the patchwork piece to be inset along one side of the angle, matching the corners. Stitch from dot to dot.

2 Pin the inset patch down the other side of the angle. Insert the needle exactly at the point and stitch the seam. Press the seam to one side.

Right: This hand-stitched basket block is made of four diamonds, stitched into pairs. A right-angle triangle is inset between the points of the diamond at each side. The two halves of the basket top are stitched together and a square is inset between the points. The base of the basket is a large triangle set above a half-square triangle. The block is completed with two rectangular units and the whole block is set on point.

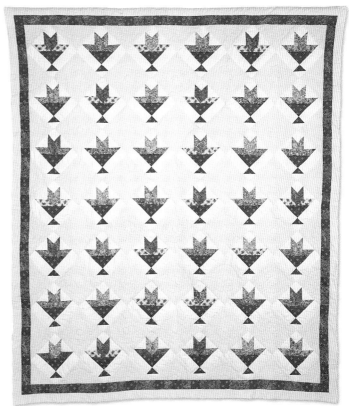

Left: This basket design is similar to the one above, except here the base of the basket is made of three half-square triangles.

Joining curved seams

Curvilinear designs are more difficult to sew than straight seams because the two edges of the curved seam do not lie flat for sewing. One seam has to be pinned and eased on to the other. To make this process easier, the curved edge should be cut on the bias. Place the straight sides of the template on the straight grain of the fabric and the curve is likely to be on the bias.

Drunkard's Path

This is one of many patchwork designs made from the same two-piece patch. It is made from 16 identical squares, each with a small contrasting quarter-circle in one corner. The patches can be arranged to create different patchwork designs, (see below and right). In the United Kingdom the patches are traditionally arranged to make the design called Robbing Peter to Pay Paul.

1 Trace and cut out the template provided. Cut the template into two along the marked arc. Fold the pieces on the diagonal through the curved arc and mark the centre line on each piece. Mark the quarter points to each side of the centre line.

2 Place each template on a different colour fabric.

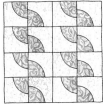

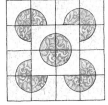

3 Keeping the straight edges along the grain of the fabric, draw around each template. Add the seam allowance and cut out. Cut notches at each mark along the curves to make matching easier.

4 With right sides together and the quarter-circle to the top, match the notches and pin, easing the fabric to fit. Use as many pins as necessary to get a smooth line.

5 Work two or three tiny back stitches and then sew tiny running stitches along the curved line. Cut the rest of the pieces and stitch them together to make 16 squares.

Right: This variation entitled "Flowers on the Drunkard's Path" combines machine piecing, machine appliqué and machine quilting.

6 If stitching by machine, pin the curved edge with the larger piece on top as this makes the fabric easy to control. Work slowly, removing the pins as you reach them. Press the seam towards the larger piece.

7 Arrange the squares to form the required pattern. Sew the squares into rows. Press the seams in adjacent rows in opposite directions. Pin the rows with right sides together matching the seams carefully. Stitch together to form the completed block.

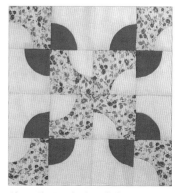

Above: The Drunkard's Path design is more complicated to piece together because of the curved patches.

English crazy patchwork

Crazy patchwork is unlike any other form of patchwork because it does not use a template. Irregular patchwork pieces are simply arranged in a pleasing way on a foundation fabric and stitched down. As a result, no two crazy patchwork quilts are ever the same.

The origin of crazy patchwork is uncertain, but most people believe it evolved from the practice of patching worn bedcovers. Eventually, after many patches had been added, the effect was like an irregular patchwork quilt. Crazy patchwork reached the height of its popularity in Britain and America in the late nineteenth century when furnishing styles were decorative and very opulent. Irregular pieces were cut from exquisite silks and velvet and the finished patchwork was richly embellished with beads, ribbons, lace and embroidery.

Crazy patchwork quilts are rarely padded and never quilted because of the difficulty of sewing through the foundation fabric. Instead, the patchwork is lined and tied, then bound. Large crazy patchwork quilts are difficult to handle while sewing. It is easier to make small blocks that can be set together to make a large quilt.

Above: Crazy patchwork is always embellished with traditional hand embroidery stitches.

1   Cut a piece of calico slightly larger than required for the foundation. This can be the size of the finished piece or about 30cm/12in square for a block as shown here. Cut the first irregular-shaped piece of fabric and baste it in one corner of the foundation. Choose fabrics of a similar weight and avoid scraps that are beginning to show signs of wear.

3   Work an embroidery stitch such as herringbone, feather or chain stitch along each seam of the patchwork. Use an embroidery thread such as stranded cotton or coton à broder on cotton fabrics, and crewel wool (yarn) or coton perlé for velvet and other heavy fabrics.

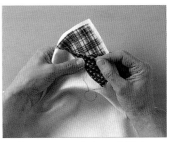

2   Pin on a second piece of fabric, overlapping the first by 5–12mm/ $^{1}/_{4}$–$^{1}/_{2}$in. The amount of overlap will depend on the thickness of the fabric and whether it frays easily. Turn under the raw edge of the second piece where it overlaps the first. Hem stitch the folded edge to the foundation through all layers. Continue to add pieces until the entire area is covered.

4   Embroider the individual patchwork shapes with isolated stitches and small, ornate embroidery motifs. The finished patchwork can also be embellished with ribbons, beads, lace and other small treasures.

Above and left: Crazy patchwork reached the height of its popularity in Victorian England, when opulent velvets, brocades and thick, silk fabrics were fashionable. It is unlikely that these quilts would have been used as bedcovers, since the highly elaborate nature of their surface decoration would render them unsuitable. Instead they would be used as throws for furniture.

Crazy patchwork can be totally random, with the entire surface covered with a hotchpotch of patches, or it can be worked in small block size pieces, and the blocks stitched together at the end. Old examples of crazy patchwork frequently have other well-known blocks such as Log Cabin designs incorporated into their scheme. These quilts may well have been samplers used to test out ideas or to learn how to stitch patchwork.

Hand embroidery stitches

The irregular shapes of Victorian crazy patchwork were invariably outlined with embroidered border stitches. Herringbone stitch, chain stitch and feather stitch were especially popular. Individual stitches such as French knots and bullion knots would then be used to decorate individual patches. Many different kinds of thread (floss) were used and "found" objects were frequently stitched into the patches.

Buttonhole stitch and blanket stitch

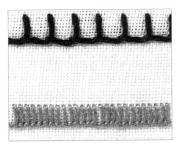

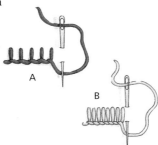

Buttonhole and blanket stitch are essentially the same, except for the way they are spaced. The space between each blanket stitch matches the length of the vertical stitch (A). With buttonhole stitch, the stitches are worked close together (B).

Work both stitches from left to right. Space the stitches as required, pulling the needle through over the top of the working thread (floss).

Closed buttonhole stitch

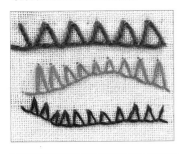

Closed buttonhole stitch is a variation of buttonhole or blanket stitch. Rows of stitching can be worked back-to-back or interlocking, to form borders or filling patterns.

Work the first blanket stitch at an angle and then work the second stitch into the same hole to make a triangle. Try working three or even four threads into the same holes for a more complex result.

Knotted buttonhole stitch

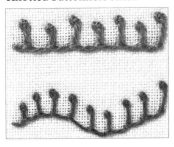

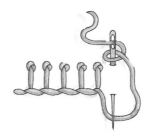

Knotted buttonhole stitch is a pretty variation of blanket stitch. Use a round thread to enhance the raised appearance of the stitch.

Working from left to right, wind the thread over your left thumb and drop the loop on to the fabric so that the tail is underneath. Push the needle through the loop and make a blanket stitch. Tug the loop tight before pulling the needle through.

Feather stitch

The Victorians often used this delicate stitch on crazy patchwork because its light, feathery line contrasted beautifully with the heavy, ornate fabrics they favoured. It can be worked as a straight or a gently curving line.

Work slanting stitches alternately to the left and to the right, as shown. Tuck the working thread (floss) under the needle before pulling it through.

Double feather stitch

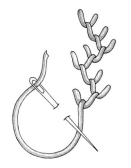

Double feather stitch forms a wide branched line that can be worked in a soft curve. It creates a delicate lacy effect when used as a filling stitch.

It is worked in the same way as feather stitch, except several stitches are made to each side before changing direction. You can either work an equal number of stitches on each side or vary the number to create an undulating line.

Bullion knot

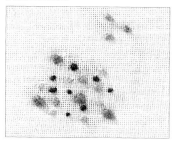

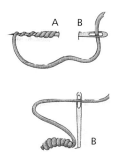

Use a long needle with a small eye to work bullion knots.

Bring the needle out at A and make a back stitch the required length of the knot (B). Bring the needle back out at A. Coil the thread round the needle seven times and pull the needle through the coil. Hold the coil down with the left thumb, pull the working thread to make the coil lie flat, then insert the needle at B.

French knot

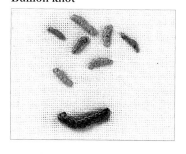

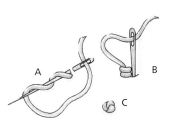

French knots add texture and colour when scattered over fabric and can also be used *en masse* to fill a shape with subtle shading and rich texture.

Bring the needle and thread up through the fabric. Take a small stitch where the thread emerged. Twist the thread around the needle twice (A) and then gently pull the needle through (B). Stitch back through the fabric at the side of the knot (C).

Cretan stitch

Cretan stitch is a long-armed feather stitch that is often used as a border pattern. It can be used singly or in rows as a filling stitch.

Begin at the top of the centre stitching line. Make long stitches down the fabric, slanting them alternately to the left and to the right. Loop the thread (floss) under the needle each time before pulling it through.

Open Cretan stitch

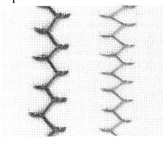

Open Cretan stitch can be worked in a straight or a gently curving line. Several rows side by side form a delicate honeycomb pattern.

Work in the same way as Cretan stitch. Keep the needle horizontal and take a small stitch towards the centre line. Pull the needle through over the working thread. Work a series of stitches alternately to the left and to the right down the fabric.

Chain stitch

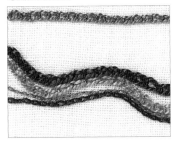

Chain stitch is one of the most popular embroidery stitches. It can be worked in a single line, in a spiral or in multiple rows to fill shapes.

Work the stitch as shown in the diagram, making each loop a similar size. Any embroidery thread suitable for the fabric can be used, but a smooth thread shows the loops well. Finish the chain by making a tiny straight stitch through the last loop.

Feathered chain stitch

Feathered chain stitch is a variation of chain stitch. Rows of feathered chain stitch can be worked side by side as a diamond or irregular filling stitch, or overlapped in a random fashion to build texture.

Make a diagonal chain stitch then make a small diagonal stitch downwards from right to left, ready to work the chain stitch on the other side. Continue down the fabric.

Herringbone stitch

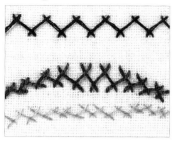

Herringbone stitch forms a crossed zigzag and makes an open border.

Working from left to right, bring the needle up through the fabric. Make a small stitch from right to left slightly ahead and above. Move down to the lower line and work a second small stitch from right to left, ahead of your last stitch. Continue alternating between the upper and lower guidelines.

Threaded herringbone stitch

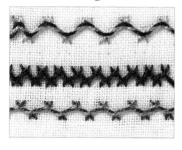

Threaded herringbone stitch produces a zigzag or solid border. Multiple rows of this stitch can be used as a very ornate filling stitch.

First, work a row of herringbone stitch. Then starting on the left-hand side, use a tapestry needle to slip the second thread (floss) first under and then over at the point where the herringbone stitches form a cross. Do not pull the thread tight.

Double herringbone stitch

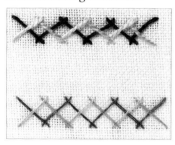

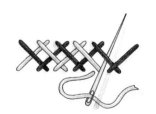

Double herringbone stitch is also used as a foundation for more complicated border stitches.

Work a row of herringbone stitches. Work a second herringbone row on top in the gaps between the stitches. You can interlace the stitches if preferred by threading the needle under the foundation row on the upward stitch and running the thread over it on the downward stitch.

Chevron stitch

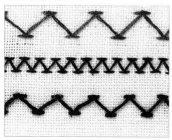

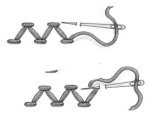

Chevron stitch looks similar to herringbone stitch. It is commonly used in smocking to make diamonds.

Bring the needle out through the fabric. Make a diagonal stitch bringing the needle out a short distance back (A). Take a stitch along the line, ending ahead of the diagonal. Work a back stitch bringing the needle back out next to the diagonal (B). Work the next diagonal stitch across to the lower line, bringing the needle out further back along the line as before.

Log Cabin designs

This design represents the walls of a cabin built from logs. The centre square is usually red to signify the fire glowing and is often known as the chimney. The light and dark sides of the block represent the firelight shining on the cabin walls.

Log Cabin patchwork has infinite variations, not only in the way the strips are cut and pieced, but also in the way the blocks are sewn together. It is always stitched together without sashing, and the most common variations are Light and Dark, Barn Raising and Straight Furrow.

Even if you decide not to use red for the centre, use the same colour throughout to unify the quilt design.

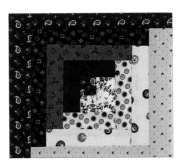

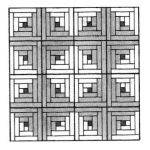

Light and Dark is formed by sewing together groups of four blocks with the dark corners to the centre.

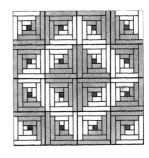

Barn Raising radiates out from the centre in alternating light and dark diamonds.

Above: This Barn Raising quilt has been made from 100 Log Cabin blocks. Each block is made of folded strips of satin, silk and cotton.

Top: A single Log Cabin block. Choose small-scale patterns or solid colours in light and dark tones for the best effect.

Straight Furrow is a strong diagonal pattern with light and dark bands.

Piecing a Log Cabin block

The size of the finished block will depend on the width of strips that you use. A standard strip is 4cm/1½in wide. Add a 12mm/½in seam allowance on each strip. The most common way to sew Log Cabin is on to a foundation fabric. Choose a fabric similar in weight and fibre content to the patchwork fabric, so that they will wash and handle in the same way. A medium-weight calico is a suitable fabric. A standard block has nine strips across the block, so if your finished strips are 2.5cm/1in wide, cut a 24cm/9¼in square.

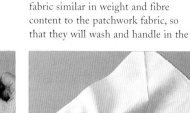

1   Plan the block by cutting 9mm/ ⅜in strips of light and dark fabric in a mixture of toning shades. Cut equal numbers of light and dark shades for each block. For a standard block you will need four different light and dark shades, which are cut into different sizes and arranged around the centre.

2   Cut the foundation fabric square. Fold it in quarters diagonally, then baste along the crease lines. Cut a 4cm/1½in square from the fabric for the centre and baste it, right side up, in the centre of the foundation. The corners of the centre square should touch the basted crease lines.

3   Pin the first light fabric strip on top of the centre square, with right sides together, matching the right-hand raw edges. Machine stitch carefully over the pins 5mm/¼in from the edges. Trim the strip level with the left-hand side of the centre square, open flat and press.

4   Pin the second strip of this fabric along the top edge of both the first two pieces. Machine stitch 5mm/¼in from the edge to the end of the squares and trim off the excess.

5   Continue in this way, alternately adding two dark and two light strips. Trim and press open the strips every time you sew and turn the foundation fabric square around ready to add the next strip. The diagonals of the Log Cabin block will only line up when it is a square, but they are a useful guide to make sure the strips are being sewn on to the foundation fabric accurately.

6   Make sufficient blocks to complete the quilt and arrange as required before sewing together. Sew the finished blocks together without sashing strips. Hand quilting is rather difficult with the foundation fabric method because of the extra layer of fabric. Instead, use tie quilting at each corner and in the centre of each block, and finish with a simple binding. Alternatively Log Cabin can be machine quilted "in-the-ditch" between each log.

Pineapple Log Cabin

Unlike the other types of Log Cabin patchwork, Pineapple Log Cabin is easier to sew from templates than from strips. This design is also known as Windmill Blades. The strips are cut in the shape of a triangle with its top sliced off, and radiate out from the centre in light and dark bands.

Plan the order of the different fabrics and trace pattern pieces for each one. If you are stitching by machine, add a 5mm/¹/₄in seam allowance all around each strip before cutting out the templates. Draw around the pattern pieces on the wrong side of the fabric and cut them out. Keep the pieces in order and label them if you are making a lot of blocks, so that you know which strip to add next.

1 Pin the first two triangles to opposite sides of the square, with right sides together and stitch using 5mm/¹/₄in seam allowances. Open out the triangles and press flat. Pin the other two triangles to the other sides of the square and stitch. Open out the triangles and press flat to form a square. Trim the seam allowances at each stage as required.

2 Pin two matching triangles from the next layer to opposite sides of the new square. Use the edges of the square as a guide when pinning and stitching the triangles in place to keep the pieces exactly in line. Stitch as before and press flat. Pin and stitch the other two triangles, then press flat.

3 Begin to add the strips, sewing two strips to opposite sides and press them flat before adding the other two. Use the previous join as a guideline as well as the raw edge to keep the block as straight as possible while sewing.

4 Continue building up the block in this way, adding the cut pieces in the correct order and alternating between light and dark shades in each group of four. Finally, add a large triangle to each corner and press flat.

5 For the best effect, join the pineapple blocks without sashing. The complete design only becomes obvious once several blocks have been stitched together. Quilt each seam with "in-the-ditch" or outline quilting and finish with a simple binding.

Above: Strips of a Pineapple Log Cabin block radiate out from the centre in light and dark fabrics.

Above: The Pineapple Log Cabin looks effective when worked in just two contrasting colours.

Below: This multi-coloured silk Courthouse Steps design has no wadding or quilting.

OTHER LOG CABIN-TYPE DESIGNS

The appearance of the basic Log Cabin block can be altered by changing the stitching order of the strips, or by varying the width of the logs.

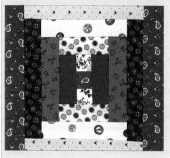

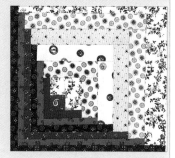

COURTHOUSE STEPS
This design is built up by sewing the two light and two dark strips on opposite sides of the central square instead of adjacent to each other.

OFF-CENTRE LOG CABIN
This design is formed from strips cut in two different widths. Cut one set of strips 4cm/1½in wide and the other set 2.5cm/1in wide. Set the blocks together so that they form wavy lines.

Seminole patchwork

Around the beginning of the twentieth century, traders supplied the Seminole Indians of Florida with hand-wheel sewing machines. Using this new equipment the Seminole people devised a unique strip patchwork that can only be worked by machine. Seminole patchwork uses vivid colours with strong contrasts which make even tiny pieces quite distinct.

The basic technique of Seminole patchwork is to sew strips of fabric together. These stitched panels are cut straight or diagonally into strips. The new strips are then rearranged and stitched to form intricate panels.

Above: Strips of Seminole patchwork can be sewn together without sashing for a very dazzling effect, or they can be broken up by sashing strips. Black fabric sets off the bright colours and patterns very effectively.

Cutting the strips

1   Fold the fabric in half lengthways, matching the selvages and steam press the layers. Place the fabric on the cutting mat. Align one of the crossways markings on the ruler with the top folded edge. Hold the ruler firmly and hold the blade of the rotary cutter against the ruler edge. Roll the blade up and down to trim the raw edge of the fabric.

2   Turn the fabric around so that the cut edge is to the left. Use the markings on the ruler to cut the width of strip you require plus 12mm/½in seam allowance.

3   Keep moving the ruler across the fabric to cut as many strips as required, remembering that each strip has four layers.

The chequerboard

1   From each of two contrasting fabrics, cut one strip 4cm/1½in wide. Sew the strips together. Press the seam to one side. Cut the strips into pieces 4cm/1½in wide.

2   With right sides together, pin the pieces together so that the seams face in opposite directions and one colour is on top of a different colour. Sew the pieces together into a chequerboard.

Joining three strips

1   Cut one strip from each of three colours, making the centre strip narrower than the other two. Join the strips together and press the seams in one direction. Cut the strip at an angle and then cut diagonal strips of equal width from the band of fabric.

2   Pin the pieces together with right sides facing. Pin carefully so that the top edge of one centre strip touches the bottom edge of the next. Stitch with a 5mm/¼in seam allowance and press the seams in the same direction.

3   Place the panel on the cutting mat and trim a long edge straight. Turn the strip around and line the grid lines up against the raw edge to cut a straight panel.

Joining five strips

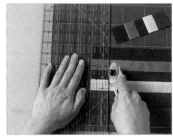

1   Cut five differently coloured fabric strips the same width and stitch them together. Press the seams in the same direction. Cut the panel into strips the same width as the original strip.

2   Pin the strips right sides together. Stagger the strips and match the seams. Stitch, then press the seams in the same direction.

3   Place the panel flat on the cutting mat and trim the triangles from one edge. Turn the strip around and line the grid lines up against the raw edge to cut a straight panel.

Joining two sets of strips

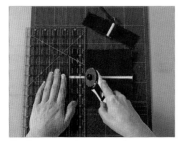

1   Cut five strips – three wide and two narrow – from two fabrics. Stitch together alternating the colours. Trim the raw edges and cut into fairly wide strips. Press the seams flat.

2   Cut two wide strips and one narrow one from two contrasting fabrics. Sew them into a second panel the same width as the first. Trim the end and cut into narrower strips.

3   Pin the strips together, staggering them so that the second seam of the first panel matches the first seam of the second panel. Sew the seams and press in one direction. Trim the edges.

Hand-stitched appliqué

Appliqué takes its name from the French verb "appliquer" meaning "to apply". The technique involves cutting fabric to shape and sewing it on to a background fabric. Appliqué has evolved into a highly decorative art and is used in various forms all over the world. The people of Hawaii and Laos, for example, stitch intricate forms of reverse appliqué, and in North America wonderful pictorial appliqué is sewn.

Raw-edge appliqué

Use this method for non-fray fabrics such as felt, or to give a ragged look to raw edges. Iron lightweight interfacing to the wrong side of woven fabrics before cutting out, or iron the appliqué to the main fabric with fusible bonding web.

Felt appliqué looks particularly effective if blanket stitch or another embroidery stitch is worked around the edge of each piece.

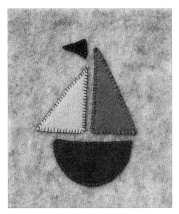

Above: Felt always has a neat trimmed raw edge that does not fray. For this reason it is a good choice for beginners.

Alternatively, you may choose to make a feature of frayed raw edges, choosing fabrics such as scrim or other loosely woven fabrics that fray easily.

1 Cut templates to the size of the finished shapes. Pin each to your choice of fabric. Cut out shapes without seams and pin them to the background fabric.

2 To stab stitch around the edge of the appliqué, bring a threaded needle up through the fabric next to the appliqué. Take it back down catching the edge of the appliqué.

Traditional appliqué

Choose simple shapes for appliqué because it is difficult to turn under raw edges on intricate shapes and keep lines smooth on tight curves. Cut motifs so that the grain matches the main fabric. Appliqué can be worked with or without an embroidery hoop. Sew the appliqué carefully to avoid fabric distortion.

1 Cut a template to the finished size and draw around it on the right side of the fabric. Cut out, adding a 5mm/¼in seam allowance all around.

2 Clip into the seam on inward-facing curves, and notch outward-facing curves. Cut up to the marked line, but not beyond it. Straight edges do not need clipping.

3 Pin the appliqué in place. Baste 12mm/½in in from the raw edge. Turn under the raw edge with the needle tip so that the pencil line disappears. Hem stitch along the fold.

Using freezer paper

Freezer paper is a wax-coated paper that is used to wrap food. The paper sticks firmly, but temporarily, to fabric if pressed with a medium iron. It is non-stain and can be peeled off easily.

1 Cut a template the exact size of the appliqué and draw around it on the dull side of the freezer paper. Cut out the shape along the lines.

2 Iron the shape to the wrong side of the fabric and cut out, adding a 5mm/¼in seam allowance all around.

Above: Strips and squares of brightly coloured fabric have been applied to a dark ground. The appliqué squares have been frayed and over-stitched with free-style machine embroidery.

3 Snip inward-facing curves close to the paper and make a notch in the seam of outward-facing curves. Turn under the raw edge and baste. Press again. The wax on the freezer paper will help the shape retain a crisp, neat edge.

4 Pin the shape in place on the background fabric and hem stitch in place. Use a small, fine needle threaded with a colour to match the appliqué or background fabric.

5 Hem most of the way around the shape, then remove the basting stitches. Slide your finger between the freezer paper and the appliqué and ease the paper out carefully. Hem the last section of the appliqué in place.

Machine appliqué

Machine appliqué is a quick and easy way to apply shapes to a background fabric. For a smooth, unpuckered finish, the fabric shape must be fixed in place before sewing. The easiest way to do this is with fusible bonding web, which will give a neat fixed shape without pin or needle marks. Machine appliqué can be worked with the presser foot in place or by free machine stitching.

Using fusible bonding web

First back the background fabric with iron-on lightweight or mediumweight interfacing or fabric stabilizer to prevent puckering when stitching over the raw edge of the fabric. The excess stabilizer can be torn away when the appliqué is complete. The interfacing will remain in place.

Fusible bonding web is sold in narrow strips or in large sheets. It is a thin mesh of glue backed with paper that is used to attach the pieces of fabric smoothly and cleanly.

1   Cut a piece of interfacing to fit the background fabric. Fix to the wrong side using a hot iron. If the fabric is unsuitable for interfacing, use fabric stabilizer instead.

2   Place the appliqué template right side down on the shiny paper side of the fusible bonding web. Trace around the template.

3   Place fusible bonding web, shiny paper side up on the wrong side of your fabric choice. Press with a medium-hot iron. Allow to cool, then cut out the shape along the lines.

4   Peel off the paper backing and press the shape in your chosen position on the background fabric, using a hot iron.

5   Set the stitch width to medium satin stitch and loosen the top tension slightly. Stitch around the edge of the shape. For a wider line, stitch on top of the first narrow zigzag.

6   Machine embroider details such as stems and veins. Here, the stem is worked in satin stitch and the veins with a straight stitch.

Above: This clever design is made of plain
and patched blocks set on-point. The
blocks have been carefully planned to
create a three-dimensional effect. The
cyclist has been appliquéd to the pieced
ground and attached with very closely
worked machine satin stitch.

Baltimore quilt

An appliqué quilt was kept for best because of all the work that went into it and also because it wasn't as hard wearing as a patchwork quilt. The finest quilts were made by women in the Baltimore area. The beautiful wreaths, garlands and baskets of flowers that adorned these nineteenth-century quilts have become standard appliqué designs. These are built up in stages because pieces overlap and are generally complex.

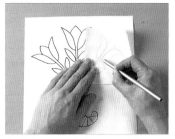

1   Enlarge the design provided and transfer it by your choice of method to the right side of the centre of the fabric. Trace the various shapes on to the shiny side of freezer paper. (To reverse the design, trace it on to the dull side instead.) Cut out the shapes.

2   Iron each freezer paper shape to the wrong side of the required fabric. Cut each shape out, adding a 5mm/¼in seam allowance all around. Notch outward-facing curves and snip inward-facing curves. Trim points carefully to reduce bulk.

3   Determine the stitching order for each section of the design. All the pieces in the background should be stitched first.

4   Slip stitch the shapes in place, using the point of the needle to turn under a 5mm/¼in hem. Match the thread to the appliqué or use a dark neutral shade such as grey.

5   The Cornucopia is formed from 12mm/½in strips of fabric sewn together in bands of light, medium and dark fabric. Cut out and pin in position on the background fabric. Turn under the edge and slip stitch in place. Press from the right side with a damp cloth.

Above: The Cornucopia is a traditional favourite design representative of plenty and prosperity. Use your choice of appliqué method to attach it neatly and accurately to the background.

Broderie perse

Broderie perse is a technique of cutting motifs from one fabric, rearranging them, and stitching them on to a new background fabric. The technique developed in the seventeenth and eighteenth centuries as a means of making precious fragments of fabric last longer.

Above: A hand-appliquéd and hand-quilted Baltimore tablerunner.

Designs were originally made using the brightly coloured chintz fabrics imported from India. When the English government imposed a ban on these fabrics to protect its own textile industry, the technique increased in popularity. In nineteenth-century America special fabrics were printed with suitable motifs for broderie perse.

1   Wash and press the fabric. Cut around the appliqué shape, leaving a 5mm/¼in seam allowance. Do not cut tiny details – these can be added at a later stage. Clip into the seam allowance to make it easier to turn under the edge. Notch outward-facing curves. Do not cut more than 3mm/⅛in into the seam allowance.

3   Sew all the pieces of appliqué in place, then press from the right side with a damp cloth. Embroider any details needed to complete the design.

2   Pin the shape in position on the background. Thread a needle with a colour to match the appliqué. Use the point of the needle to turn under the edge and slip stitch in place with small, almost invisible stitches.

Below: Traditional broderie perse designs incorporated exotic floral motifs.

Shadow appliqué

Shadow appliqué is simple to work. Brightly coloured fabric is sandwiched between a sheer top layer and a base fabric. The sheer top and base are traditionally white, but subtle and unusual effects can be achieved by using different colours instead. The appliqué design needs to be strongly coloured to allow for the effect when the sheer top layer is placed over it.

1 Make a template of the design provided. Trace each shape on to fusible bonding web. Draw the shapes in groups according to the colour of fabric that will be used.

2 Iron the bonding web on to the wrong side of the fabric, following the manufacturer's instructions. Cut out the shapes along the lines. Peel off the backing paper.

3 Place the background fabric over the template. Place the shapes on the fabric using the template as a guide. Cover the shapes with a muslin cloth and carefully press to secure them.

4 Place a sheer fabric such as voile, organdie or organza on top and pin in place. If you want to quilt the appliqué, add wadding (batting) and backing under the base fabric at this stage.

5 Work small running stitches close to the appliqué, through all layers. Stitch around every shape even if it is overlapping or sitting on top of another. Once the appliqué is complete, details such as leaf veins can be worked in running stitch.

Above: Shadow appliqué can be as simple or as complex as you make it.

Hawaiian appliqué

This colourful and intricate form of appliqué has been practised by the people of Hawaii since the early nineteenth century. Several distinctive features set Hawaiian appliqué apart from other reverse appliqué designs. It is created using a paper cut-out and, when complete, it is always quilted with rows of "echo quilting", which are said to resemble the waves lapping on the shore of the people's island home.

1   Choose the size for the appliqué, then cut a paper square the size of the appliqué plus 9mm–2.2cm/³/₈–⁷/₈in. Fold it in quarters, then in half diagonally so that the folded edges are together. Draw a snowflake pattern between the two folded edges. Draw the border pattern across the edge. Cut out the pattern, but do not discard the outside piece.

2   Hawaiian appliqué quilts are traditionally made in two solid colours, typically vivid hues of red, blue, green or orange on a white ground. Cut one piece of coloured fabric and one piece of white fabric slightly larger than the pattern. Place the coloured fabric on top of the white fabric and position the opened pattern in the centre.

3   Carefully draw around the edge with a sharp, soft pencil. Draw the border outline in the same way using the other piece. With small stitches, baste 5mm/¹/₄in inside the marked lines of the main motif through both layers of fabric. Baste 5mm/¹/₄in outside the border line.

4   Cut out the appliqué from the top fabric, one section at a time, along the marked lines using small, pointed scissors. To make the fabric easier to turn under, snip into any corners and along deep curves. Make these small cuts no deeper than 3mm/¹/₈in.

5   Use the point of the needle to turn under 3mm/¹/₈in along the raw edge. Sew the folded edge of the appliqué to the main fabric with tiny, close slip stitches. Work around all the edges until the entire appliqué is stitched in place. Stitch the inside edge of the border in the same way.

6   Remove all the basting and press the right side of the panel with a damp cloth. Add a thin layer of wadding (batting) and a backing to the back, then work a row of outline quilting around the appliqué. Echo quilt the entire design with lines 5–15mm/¹/₄–⁵/₈in apart.

Stained glass appliqué

The bright, bold colours and the simple shapes used in stained glass windows are ideal for appliqué design. With this technique, shapes are held together with a narrow fabric strip. In recent years stained-glass appliqué has become so popular that narrow sticky-back bias tape has been produced especially for this task. This tape is available in a range of colours as well as the traditional black.

The finished appearance of stained glass appliqué relies on a distinct contrast between the shapes and the bias tape. Plain fabric in bold colours are guaranteed to work, but you can use fabrics with a subtle pattern. There are many new patchwork fabrics that have a self-coloured print in a slightly darker shade that are suitable. These fabrics can be used to emulate the rough texture of old stained glass windows. There are books with hundreds of stained glass designs to give you inspiration or choose a simple design such as the Charles Rennie Mackintosh rose below for your first attempt.

Right: Choose designs with strong lines and clear colours for stained glass appliqué.

1 Make a template on tracing paper and transfer to the right side of the background fabric using your choice of methods. Draw curves in an outward motion to produce a smoother line.

2 Decide where all the colours will go and mark this on a copy of the template. Cut the template along the lines to separate the pieces.

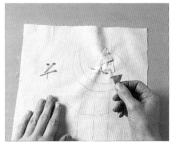

3 Pin the template shapes on the right side of the appropriate colour fabric and cut out. Beginning in the centre of the design, pin the first few pieces of appliqué on the background.

Above: This classic Arab seven-pointed star pattern has been worked in traditional colours. Over 230 metres/250 yards of handmade bias binding outlines the stars.

4 Cut lengths of bias tape to fit over the edges of the appliqué and pin in place. Fold under the end of each piece of tape and cover the end of the last piece. Continue in this way, pinning and basting the appliqué.

5 Cover the appliqué with a muslin cloth and press with a steam iron to secure the tape. If the design is to be used as a picture, stitching is unnecessary. Otherwise, slip stitch along both sides of the binding.

Reverse appliqué

With reverse appliqué, instead of adding pieces of fabric, sections of fabric are cut away from the right side to create a design. Extra colours can be added to sections of the design to prevent the fabric layers from becoming unwieldy.

The best known reverse appliqué is the brightly coloured Molas worked by the women of the San Blas islands. These maze-like designs feature simplistic animals, birds and plants.

1   Draw and cut out a template. Choose a simple design and make narrow sections no smaller than 5mm/¼in. Transfer the design to the right side of the fabric. Draw an outline 5mm/¼in away from the design.

2   Arrange the fabrics together. In this case there are three layers: the patterned top fabric, a plain cream fabric and a white base fabric. Baste between the lines of the appliqué and around the outside of the design. Keep the lines at least 3mm/⅛in away from the marked lines.

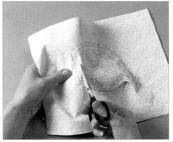

3   Using the template as a reference, cut between the lines of the appliqué motif, through the top layer of fabric only. Snip into the corners without cutting through the marked lines.

4   Find the areas that should have cream showing. Turn under the cut edge with the point of the needle and slip hem the folded edge. Notch or snip the deeper curves if required so that the fabric lies flat. If the area is wider than 12mm/½in, trim the excess fabric in the seam allowance to 5mm/¼in.

Right: Hand-worked appliqué and reverse appliqué feature in this quilt design, which has been pieced together and quilted by machine.

Left: Although only made from between two and four layers of fabric, Mola quilts are multi-coloured because the bottom layer is often pieced from several colours and other colours inserted as required.

5   In areas you want to be white, cut through the cream fabric as well to reveal the white beneath. Trim and clip the seam allowances and clip carefully into the corners.

6   Turn under both fabrics together and slip hem along the fold. Press the finished appliqué on the wrong side and then press again with a damp pressing cloth.

Above: Start with simple designs and few layers when learning reverse appliqué.

Putting it together

Patchwork and appliqué blocks can be joined together in many different ways. They can be sewn directly together, separated by strips of fabric or by both strips and setting squares. The same set of blocks will look quite different made up in these three ways.

Joining blocks

Some patchwork blocks, such as Log Cabin, are joined directly together so that the wonderful shading can be seen to full effect. Album or sampler quilts, where each block is quite distinct from the others, are usually sewn together between strips of fabric

called sashing. The different blocks may be in co-ordinating fabrics and the right sashing fabric can "pull" the colour scheme together. Often the sashing is self-coloured, but a quilt can look striking with the sashing in a busy, colourful print that contains all the colours used in the blocks. Blocks that are in similar colours or all the

same design can benefit from extra setting squares as well as sashing strips. Setting squares are the same width as the sashing and sit at the corners of each block. They are usually in a contrasting colour. Piece smaller squares and narrower strips together to make more unusual setting blocks and sashing strips.

Side by side

1 Arrange the blocks for the first row on a clean, flat surface in the correct order.

2 With right sides together, pin the first two blocks. Match the seams if possible and ease the edges to fit if required. Machine stitch the seam.

3 Continue adding blocks one at a time to complete the row. Press the seams in the same direction.

4 Complete all the rows in this way, pressing the seams of adjacent rows in opposite directions.

5 Pin the first two rows right sides together. Match the seams carefully, inserting pins along each seam line and easing the fabric in between if required. Stitch over the pins.

6 Press the seams and trim the outside edges before binding.

Using sashing

1 Determine the sashing width, and add 12mm/½in for seams. Cut sashing the length of each block. Pin and stitch horizontally between blocks.

2 Cut sashing strips to fit vertically between the quilt panels. Pin and sew the sashing in place.

3 Add sashing strips to the outside edge of the quilt before the binding.

Sashing strips and setting blocks

1 Add sashing between the horizontal rows of blocks. For the vertical rows, cut more sashing the same length as the blocks. Cut squares for setting blocks the length and width of the sashing width. Sew a square between each piece of sashing. Press the seams in to the square.

2 Pin the pieced sashing to the quilt panels, matching the seams carefully. Machine stitch using the straight edge of the sashing as a stitching guide. Add setting blocks and sashing strips around the outside edge before adding the binding.

The quilt sandwich

Once you have pieced the blocks together into a patchwork cloth, press the design carefully from the wrong side. Measure the design to make sure it is the correct size. At this point decide whether or not you will add a border all around the design. Borders can be pieced or plain, and can incorporate corner posts. They can be used to pull the whole colour scheme together, or to add accent colours.

Decide on the border width, then cut border strips the length of each side plus seam allowances. Add to opposite sides of the quilt. Measure the quilt width. Cut, then stitch the borders in place top and bottom.

2 Cut the quilt backing 5–10cm/ 2–4in larger than the quilt top, stitching lengths together as required. Cut the wadding (batting) slightly smaller than the backing. Centre the quilt top on the wadding. Smooth out any ripples with your hands.

4 If you will be hand quilting in a frame, baste the layers together. Begin in the centre and stitch out in radiating lines.

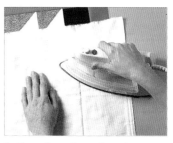

1 Press the quilt top from the wrong side, making sure that all the seams lie flat. Trim any loose threads. Turn the quilt right side up and press thoroughly with a pressing cloth to remove any puckers. Determine and transfer the quilt design at this point.

3 The quickest way to secure the layers is with pins. Ordinary safety pins are suitable, but the quilt will lie flatter with special quilting pins that have a deeper curve on the underside. Insert pins every 5–10cm/2–4in, working out from the centre.

5 If you will be quilting in a hoop or by machine, sew horizontal and vertical basting lines at 5–10cm/2–4in intervals to hold the layers securely.

Transferring a quilting design

Quilting adds the final decorative touch to a patchwork quilt, but it takes skill to make the design fit. If you are quilting a pattern, it is best to transfer the quilt design to the right side of the patchwork cloth before you make up the quilt sandwich.

Prick and pounce

1   Draw the quilting design on a sheet of firm paper. Remove the thread from the sewing machine and stitch along these lines with a long stitch. Lightly rub the wrong side of the paper to remove the rough edges and help the pounce to go through.

2   Place the template on the fabric. Make a pounce bag by putting a tablespoonful of cornflour (cornstarch) in the centre of a double layer of muslin. Draw the edges together and dab the bag all over the design.

3   Check that the design has been transferred to the fabric before lifting the template off carefully. To make the lines more permanent, mark with a sharp, soft pencil.

Dressmaker's carbon

Choose a sheet of dressmaker's carbon that closely matches the colour of the fabric but still allows you to see the design's lines once they have been transferred. Check that the marks can be removed on a spare piece of fabric.

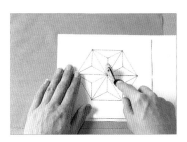

1   Place the dressmaker's carbon, coloured-side down, on the right side of the fabric. Position the template on top and trace over each line.

2   Carefully remove the dressmaker's carbon. The lines of the design should be clearly marked on the fabric.

TIPS

• Transfer the quilt design on to the right side of the fabric before you make up the quilt sandwich. That way you can press on to a hard surface and mark a clear design on the quilt top.

• Quilting "in-the-ditch" does not need marking on the surface.

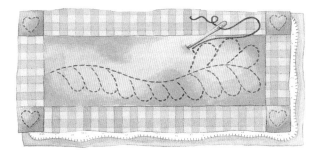

Quilting templates

There are many different quilting templates you can buy. Choose one made from translucent plastic because it will be the most hardwearing and will allow you to see exactly where you are marking.

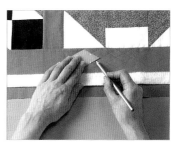

1   Position the template with the slots exactly where you want to quilt. Check that the design is positioned to go around the corner and then mark with a soft pencil. Use a colour that will just show up on the fabric or one that you can wash out.

2   Small templates can be used to mark a repeating border on a quilt. Cut two notches to show where the template must be placed each time to create the same repeat. Mark with a sharp, soft pencil in a similar colour to the fabric that will wash out.

Quilter's tape

It is not always necessary to mark out quilting lines on the quilt top. On patchwork quilts, for example, you can use the seam lines as a guide for the stitching.

This 5mm/¹/₄in wide sticky-backed tape is useful for adding seam allowances around patchwork shapes before cutting and also for marking straight quilting lines. Stick one edge of the tape exactly where you want to stitch and use it as a guideline. The tape can be lifted and re-used several times.

1   For outline quilting, where each shape is outlined with a row of running stitches 5mm/¹/₄in away from the seam line, stick the tape along the seam line.

2   Sew a line of small running stitches along the other edge of the quilter's tape.

3   For echo quilting, lift the tape and move it to the other side of the quilting stitches. Sew along the far side of the tape. Keep moving the tape further in to produce equally spaced quilting lines.

Above: The basket quilt above has been echo quilted with concentric lines around the basket handles.

Quilting

Quilting is the stitching technique used to hold layers of fabric and wadding (batting) together. You can quilt by hand or machine or simply tie the layers together. Quilting takes place after the quilt sandwich is made up and before the binding is added.

Decorative quilting

Although all quilting embellishes the surface of a quilt in some way, most people associate quilt-making with creating patterns and motifs. Amish quilts, which are made from large pieces of fabric, are famous for their intricate quilting. Decorative quilting patterns are most effective when stitched on larger pieces of plain fabric, rather than on small patchwork or appliqué squares. They are usually transferred to the quilt top with a template.

There are three types of decorative quilting patterns: medallions, borders and corners. Medallions are large, ornate motifs used mainly as a centrepiece for a quilt. Traditional patterns include the Lover's Knot and the Feather Wreath.

Border patterns are narrow, linear patterns that fit along borders and sashing strips. Small shapes such as diamonds and single feathers can be repeated to make a border pattern. Templates for borders often include a corner, to allow you to complete a border all around the quilt top.

Corner motifs are intricate, ornate motifs that often match the style of the central medallion on the quilt top. Feathers and fans are popular corner motifs.

Wholecloth quilts

For those who love hand stitching, wholecloth quilts are an excellent way to show off quilting technique. Traditionally made from cotton sateen, the surface sheen on the fabric brings out the textures formed by the quilting patterns. Traditional whole-cloth patterns, handed down through the generations, can give us an idea about who owned the quilt. Wedding quilts usually feature hearts in the border but it was considered unlucky for someone to stitch hearts in a quilt until they were at least engaged. Wholecloth quilts take careful planning. The patterns are usually symmetrical and feature medallion, border and corner motifs in an attractive design. Wales has a strong tradition of making wholecloth quilts. Welsh wedding quilts are particularly distinctive, made in bold-coloured sateen with a different colour on the underside.

Left: Wholecloth quilts will appeal to those who love hand stitching. This intricate design is worked entirely in running stitch.

Quilting by hand

Hand quilting may be time consuming but it is very relaxing and produces the softest finish on a quilt. Quilting needles are very fine and can pierce the skin quite easily, so you will need a thimble to protect the middle finger of your sewing hand. Some people also use a leather or quilting thimble on their other hand to guide the needle back through the fabric. Whether you are using a hoop or a frame, make sure you are sitting comfortably and in good light before you begin.

Below: This Carpenter's Square design is hand pieced and hand quilted.

1 Thread a small "betweens" needle (size 8) with a single length of quilting thread and tie a knot in the end. The knot must be small enough to pull through the fabric, yet large enough to catch in the wadding (batting). Take a small stitch into the quilt top and through the wadding.

2 Pull the needle through and tug the thread sharply to pull the knot through the quilt top to catch in the wadding layer.

3 Use the thimble to guide the needle at an angle through the layers and then bring the needle back

through to the surface. Take several stitches at a time along the needle before pulling the thread through. Try to make the stitches all the same size (with practice you will be able to make them smaller). The stitches will probably come out smaller and more irregular on the wrong side.

4 End the quilting with a knot tugged into the wadding. Wind the thread twice around the needle and insert it through the quilt top and wadding. Bring the needle back out on the surface and tug the thread sharply to sink the knot into the wadding. Trim the thread end.

Machine quilting

Machine quilting is much quicker than hand quilting, but the preparation should be more thorough. If the layers are not basted together carefully unsightly folds will be caught in on the underside.

1 Use a size 90/14 needle in the machine and set the stitch length to sew about 12 stitches per 2.5cm/1in. Stitch a small sample first to check the tension, using the same quilt layers. You may need to loosen the top tension so that the stitches lie flat. Fit a clear-view presser foot in the machine. This can be made of perspex or have a cut-away section at the front that allows you to see exactly where you are stitching.

2 When stitching a large quilt, you will have to roll the basted layers quite tightly and evenly to fit in the sewing machine. Machine stitch as much of the flat area as possible, then unroll the quilt ready to stitch the next section.

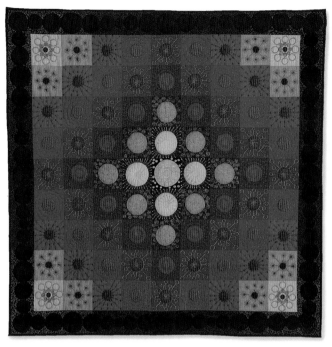

Above: Appliqué circles on a simple one-patch design have been heavily quilted using free-motion quilting.

Methods of quilting

There are many different quilting designs and most are suitable for both hand and machine stitching.

Choose a stitching pattern according to the amount of time you can spare, the type of wadding (batting) you are using and the effect you want to create. For example, patchwork quilted "in-the-ditch" is almost invisible, whereas filling patterns (such as those used in wholecloth quilts) will be a major feature of the overall design. The lines of stitching on some types of wadding should be spaced as close as every 7.5–10cm/3–4in to prevent the wadding from breaking up in the wash. Other types only need to be tied or stitched every 25cm/10in.

"In-the-ditch"
This technique is almost invisible when stitched in a matching or neutral thread. Work hand stitches in the centre of the seam line. If quilting by machine, stitch slowly and flatten the top fabric on either side of the seam so that the stitches fall exactly "in-the-ditch". Stop when you reach a corner, making sure the needle is in the fabric, lift the presser foot and turn the quilt to face down the next seam.

TIP

To make the stitches almost invisible, nylon thread can be used on the top of the machine and a 100 per cent cotton thread in the bobbin.

Selective

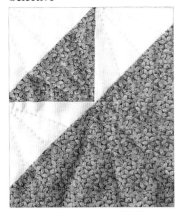

This method is most suitable for patchwork or appliqué quilts. It is used to highlight certain areas by quilting them and leaving other areas unstitched. Stitch across the seam lines to create a distinctive pattern.

Outline

Lines of outline quilting should be stitched 5mm/¹/₄in away from the seam lines and worked around every shape on the design. Use quilter's tape or a 5mm/¹/₄in ruler to keep the lines straight.

Echo

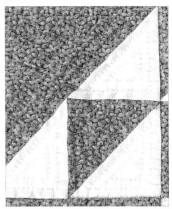

Begin echo quilting in the same way as outline quilting, and stitch further lines every 5mm/¹/₄in until the whole quilt is covered. Match the thread to the background or use a contrasting colour thread for a decorative effect.

Parallel lines

This is a quick and easy method especially if worked by machine. Score lines on the fabric with a blunt point or use a spacer bar on the machine to stitch all the lines the same distance apart.

Shell-filling pattern

Curved filling patterns are more suitable for quilting by hand. They look best stitched on sashing strips and borders, or plain fabric areas of a quilt rather than on patchwork.

Diamond-filling pattern

Straight filling patterns are ideal for machine stitching. Mark the design lines carefully. When you reach a corner, leave the needle in the fabric, lift the presser foot and turn the quilt to face along the next seam. Lower the presser foot and continue. On more complicated patterns, determine a stitching route before you begin to ensure the lines are stitched with as little stopping and starting as possible.

Trapunto quilting

This method of quilting makes use of loose stuffing rather than wadding (batting). Two layers of fabric are stitched together using a quilt design. The backing fabric is slit and the stuffing added. The padded areas stand out in relief and, for contrast, the flat areas can be covered in filling stitch. This is one of the oldest forms of quilting and was used to decorate clothes and furnishings in the seventeenth and eighteenth centuries.

Trapunto quilting was introduced to America by the early settlers and was originally worked on linsey-woolsey or cotton. In the early nineteenth century, the stitching of large, intricately patterned, all-white quilts became popular among wealthy women in the north-east and southern parts of the United States.

Use a glazed cotton or satin fabric for the top layer to emphasize the relief areas and a closely woven fabric such as calico for the wrong side. You can use a loosely woven fabric if you prefer, and use a bodkin or similar tool to stuff the padding between the woven threads, but this will not give such high relief.

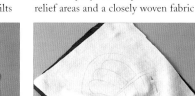

1   Trace the design directly through the backing fabric. Place the design face down and place the main fabric on top.

2   Baste around the design to hold the two layers together. Sew along all the design lines by hand or machine. Sew or tie off the ends on the wrong side.

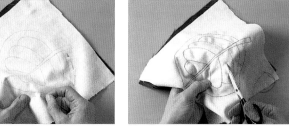

3   Using sharp embroidery scissors, cut a small slit in the first area to be stuffed. Be careful to cut only through the calico and not to cut into the main fabric.

4   Using a bodkin or similar blunt tool, push small pieces of stuffing into the slit. Use the tool to ease the stuffing into the corners and to spread it out into an even layer.

5   Sew the two cut edges together with herringbone stitch. Do not try to pull the edges close together as the raw edges will fray. Stitch into the stuffing for extra security.

Above: Padding a large area creates relief in a design, but to stop the fabric around it from puckering you will need to pad areas of the whole fabric.

Italian quilting

*Italian, or corded, quilting is a purely decorative form of quilting. No
wadding (batting) is used to make the quilt extra-warm, which explains
why it became popular in places with a warm climate, such as southern
Italy. Wool (yarn) or cord is pulled through narrow stitched channels to
produce thick raised lines on the right side. Italian quilting was very
fashionable in the seventeenth and eighteenth centuries.*

1 Trace the design on to the backing.
Place it right side down and position
the main fabric on top. Baste around
the design to hold the layers together.
Stitch along all the design lines. Sew
or tie off the ends on the wrong side.

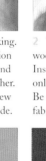

2 Thread the needle with cord or
wool (yarn) without knotting the end.
Insert the needle into the backing
only between two rows of stitching.
Be careful not to puncture the main
fabric with the needle.

3 Push the needle along the channel
as far as it will go and bring it back
out through the backing fabric. Pull
the wool through to leave a
12mm/¹/₂in tail. Insert the needle
back in the same hole and take
another stitch, leaving a small loop on
the wrong side.

4 Work around corners by taking
small stitches around the curve,
leaving loops on the wrong side.

5 Once all the channels have been
filled, pull the fabric on the bias to
even out the cord and remove any
puckers.

Above: Traditionally bedcovers and clothing
such as waistcoats and caps were richly
embellished with corded channels. Italian
quilting is often worked alongside trapunto
quilting, with the corded channels used to
echo the high-relief areas of padding.

Choose a soft, medium-weave fabric
for the backing to allow you to pull the
needle and wool (yarn) through the weave
fairly easily.

SHADOW CORDING

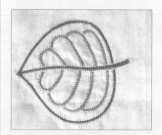

Shadow corded quilting is
worked in the same way as
Italian quilting. Choose a firm
sheer fabric such as organdie or
organza for the top layer. Insert
brightly coloured cord or wool
(yarn) through the channels.

Sashiko quilting

This traditional Japanese quilting technique became widely known in the early eighteenth century, when women made warm outdoor jackets by sewing two layers of indigo-dyed fabric together with rows of neatly worked running stitches.

Initially Sashiko quilting stitches were purely functional, but later they were stitched in complex geometric patterns. Although it incorporates a traditional embroidery stitch, Sashiko is ideal for quilting with a thin layer of wadding (batting) between the main fabric and backing. As with all things Japanese, the patterns are formal with strict guidelines for stitching. Use special Sashiko thread (floss), coton à broder or fine coton perlé for stitching, and keep to the same number of stitches per 2.5cm/1in – usually just five, six or seven evenly-sized stitches.

1 Transfer the design to the top fabric. Try to sew the pattern in continuous lines instead of stopping and starting. Look closely at the pattern before you start to determine the best route to take.

2 Two of the running stitches should never come together at a point. Leave spaces at corners and stop lines short of each other if they are going to finish at the same central point.

Above: Sashiko worked on the traditional blue ground but with shades of white and pale blue stitching.

TRADITIONAL SASHIKO PATTERNS

Maru Bishamon, a Buddhist symbol, is an intricate design of interlocking circles.

Higaki (cypress fence). Cypress screens are a decorative feature in traditional Japanese houses.

Asanoha (hemp leaf). Hemp was one of the five basic crops grown in ancient Japan.

Matsukawabishi (pine bark diamond) – a symbol found in all forms of Japanese decorative art.

Tied quilting

Tied quilting is the quickest way to bind the three layers of a quilt together. It is used when the wadding (batting) is too thick, or the top layer too firm, to stitch through easily. Patchwork quilts worked on a foundation fabric, such as Log Cabin, are traditionally tied. The ties can be knotted at the front or back of the quilt, or even tied in a bow. Buttons, beads or charms can be added as a decorative feature.

1 Use long quilting pins rather than safety pins so that you can tie over the pin. The space left between the ties depends on the type of wadding (batting) used, but generally, a spacing of 7.5–15cm/3–6in will be enough. Put the ties closer together if the quilt will be washed often. If the border on the quilt is wider than 7.5cm/3in, it needs to be tied, too.

2 Thread the needle with strong thread: fine crochet cotton, coton à broder or coton perlé are all suitable. Take a back stitch directly over the pin, leaving a 7.5cm/3in tail, and then work a second back stitch on top. Trim the end, leaving the same length of tail.

3 Tie the ends in a reef knot (square knot) working left over right and then right over left. Pull the knot tight and trim the tails neatly.

4 For speed, instead of sewing and tying each knot individually, move to the next pin without cutting the thread. Work across the quilt until you run out of thread, then snip the threads and tie as before.

5 As a decorative finish, tie short tufts of cotton into the reef knot before you trim the tails. Cut small bundles of thread about 5cm/2in long and place them on top of the first knot. Tie a second knot on top and pull tight. Trim the tufts and tails evenly.

Above: Tied quilting has been used to decorate the back of this quilt, which has been pieced using the same colours, but a different design to the quilt front.

Binding a quilt

Binding is the final stage in the quilt-making process and the last opportunity to add colour and definition. There are different ways of binding a quilt. Square or rectangular quilts have binding that is cut on the straight grain while binding for curved quilts is cut on the bias.

Adding separate binding

1 Trim the wadding (batting) and backing level with the quilt top. Cut binding strips 5cm/2in wide along the lengthways grain of the fabric. Cut four strips each 2.5cm/1in longer than each side of the quilt. Piece the lengths together as required, joining the lengths on the diagonal. Along one long edge of each, turn in and press a 5mm/¼in seam allowance.

2 Pin one longer length of binding to the quilt side with right sides together and raw edges aligned. Just 12mm/½in of binding should overhang at each end. Begin stitching a seam allowance' width from the edge. Reverse stitch to secure the ends, then stitch the binding to the quilt. Stop 5mm/¼in from the corner and reverse stitch to secure the ends.

3 Pin and stitch the other pieces of binding to the quilt in the same way, stopping the stitching 5mm/¼in from each corner. Reverse stitch to secure the ends.

4 Fold the binding over the raw edges of the wadding and backing. Pin, then slip stitch the folded edge of the binding in place to the backing. The binding will be much wider on the wrong side than on the quilt front. Stitch down the binding on the sides first and then along the top and bottom edges.

5 To reduce bulk in the corners, trim excess fabric to 5mm/¼in. Fold the next binding strip over at the corner and pin in place. Slip stitch along the next edge.

Adding a fold finish

1 This simple finish is suitable for quilts that have sashing strips added to each side. Fold back the top layer of the quilt and trim the wadding (batting) by 5mm/¹⁄₄in.

2 Fold the raw edges of the backing fabric over the wadding only and baste in place.

3 Turn under 5mm/¹⁄₄in along the raw edges of the quilt top and pin so that the folded edges are together. Slip stitch the edges neatly.

Adding self binding

1 If the quilt back is at least 2.5cm/1in wider all around than the quilt top and cut in a co-ordinating fabric, a self-binding will add a very neat, slim finish.Trim the quilt top and wadding (batting) evenly. Trim the backing 2.5cm/1in larger all around. To prepare the mitred corner, fold one corner of the backing over until it touches the quilt top at the corner. Fingerpress the fold, then trim across the diagonal.

2 Turn in a 5mm/¹⁄₄in seam along the trimmed diagonal, then all around the backing. Fold the backing over again to enclose the quilt top and wadding. Check that the mitres meet neatly and pin.

3 Slip stitch the folded edge to the quilt front. Slip stitch the slit in the mitred corners to finish.

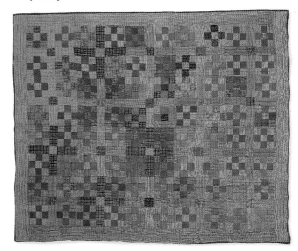

Right: This simple nine-patch Railroad design, dating from about the turn of the twentieth century, is made from the cotton shirts of the railroad workers. It is bound with two different colours.

Making continuous binding

Bias binding is cut across the diagonal of the fabric to enable it to stretch smoothly around curved edges. As you need long lengths of binding for a quilt, it is easier to stitch and cut a continuous binding rather than piecing together numerous strips of fabric.

Mitring is a very neat way to finish square corners because it reduces excess bulk and covers all the raw edges. Mitring is easier on light- or medium-weight fabric that can be pressed with a crisp foldline.

1 Cut a square of fabric with the edges on the straight grain. Cut the square in half diagonally. Pin two short edges with right sides together. Stitch 5mm/^{1}/$_4$in from the raw edge, reverse stitching at each end.

2 Press the seam open. Place the pieced fabric right side up on a flat surface. On the right side, draw parallel lines, 5cm/2in apart. Use a wide ruler and press down hard to prevent the fabric from stretching.

3 With right sides together, pin the diagonal edges to make a tube. Offset the edges so that the first line below the corner is level with the opposite edge of fabric. Stitch 5mm/^{1}/$_4$in from the raw edge. Press the seam open.

4 Cut the fabric tube into a continuous strip, beginning at one corner and cutting along the marked lines. Press the bias binding with a steam iron, pulling it slightly to remove excess stretch.

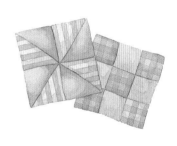

Mitring corners

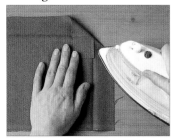

1 Turn over and press the fabric on the hem line along both sides of the corner, keeping the fold along the straight grain if possible. Turn over the corner exactly where the crease lines cross and press.

2 Open out the corner and trim across the diagonal 5mm/^{1}/$_4$in away from the pressed line. Turn over 5mm/^{1}/$_4$in along all the raw edges and press.

3 Turn the hem over along the crease lines. Check that the mitre matches and adjust if necessary, then pin and baste. Stitch close to the turned edge of the hem. Slip stitch the mitred corner.

Adding a bias binding edge

1 Trim the corners of the quilt top into a curve if required or simply tidy the raw edges. Pin the bias binding along the edge of the quilt top, easing it around the curves. Stitch in place 5mm/¼in from the raw edge.

2 Trim the wadding (batting) and backing to the same size as the quilt top. Clip carefully into any points on a decorative curved edge.

3 Turn the quilt over. Turn under 5mm/¼in along the raw edge of the binding and pin in place. Slip stitch the binding to the backing.

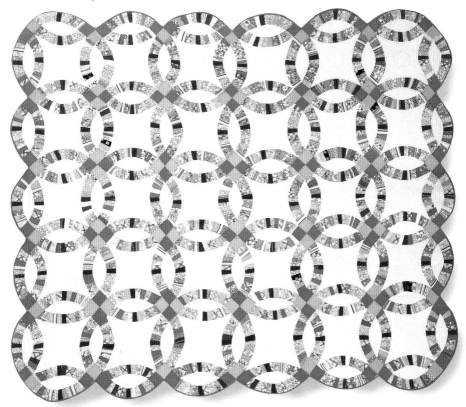

Above: This Double Wedding Ring design incorporates curved seams and is traditionally finished with a scalloped edge. This type of edge requires a separate binding cut on the bias.

Bias binding is used when the quilt has a decorative curved edge, or where a quilt is curved at the corners to hang neatly over a bed. Unlike other binding techniques, bias binding is pinned and stitched to one side –

usually the quilt front – before the wadding (batting) and backing are trimmed level. The binding has to be folded into small tucks to lie flat over the points along the edge of this Double Wedding Ring design.

The sewing machine

A sewing machine is one of the most expensive pieces of sewing equipment you will buy and you should take as much care choosing one as you would a washing machine or a car. Think about how much sewing you expect to do, not only next year but also ten or twenty years ahead.

Types of machine

All sewing machines sew a line of simple straight stitches, but new technology means there are many different types on the market.

Basic straight stitch and zigzag
The only basic straight stitch machines around today are antiques – but they still form beautiful stitches. Zigzag stitches move the needle from side to side. The stitch width and spacing can be altered.

Automatic
Automatic machines can move the fabric backwards and forwards while stitching to produce stretch stitches, saddle stitch and overlocking. They have special discs inside called pattern cams that produce a variety of elaborate embroidery stitches.

Electronic
Electronic machines (above) are smoother and more sophisticated than ordinary automatic machines. The motor is controlled electronically and stops as soon as you lift your foot from the pedal. The machine can also sew very slowly if required with the same power. Electronic machines can be automatic or computerized, having either cams or a computer to create the stitches.

Computerized
Computerized machines (above) are advanced models with silicon chips instead of pattern cams and are capable of a huge range of ornamental stitches. The stitches can be more complicated because the fabric can move in all directions. Touch-button panels or screens make them simple to use and some can stitch small motifs, or your own embroidery designs when linked to a personal computer.

CHOOSING A SEWING MACHINE

Most people only ever use the straight stitch and zigzag on a sewing machine so think carefully before spending a lot of money on technology you don't really need. If you intend to make soft furnishings and curtains, a sturdy, second-hand flatbed machine may be best. Free-arm machines have a narrow arm that extends above the base to allow fabric to be moved around. They are more suitable for dressmaking.

Take samples of different fabrics such as jersey, silk and denim with you and try them out folded double on the machines. Check that threading up is easy and the bobbin case is not difficult to handle. Check that the electric fittings and attachments are well made.

Find out what accessories are included and if parts are easily replaced. Finally check that the machine packs away easily and isn't too heavy. After all, they're supposed to be portable.

Spend some time reading the manual and becoming familiar with the different parts. If you haven't used a sewing machine before, practise sewing on paper without thread first. For this, set all the dials at zero except for the stitch length, which should be between 2 and 3. Using lined paper, go up and down the lines, then try stopping and reversing, and very slowly, following curves and circles. Once you are comfortable, practise the same techniques on a double layer of gingham fabric.

Know your machine

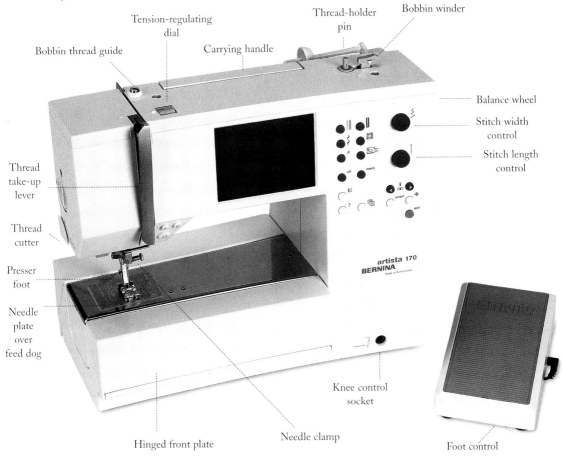

Tension-regulating dial

Bobbin thread guide

Carrying handle

Thread-holder pin

Bobbin winder

Balance wheel

Stitch width control

Stitch length control

Thread take-up lever

Thread cutter

Presser foot

Needle plate over feed dog

artista 170
BERNINA
Made in Switzerland

Knee control socket

Hinged front plate

Needle clamp

Foot control

Balance wheel
This controls the sewing machine. On manual machines, turn the wheel to lower the needle.

Bobbin winder
This allows you to fill the bobbin quickly and evenly.

Foot control/knee contol
This starts, stops and controls the speed that the machine stitches.

Needle clamp
This secures the shaft of the needle into the machine.

Needle plate
The needle plate surrounds the feed teeth and has a hole for the needle.

Presser foot
This holds the fabric flat on the needle plate so that a stitch can form.

Stitch length control
Use this to alter the length of straight stitch and the density of zigzag stitch.

Stitch width control
This controls the amount the needle moves sideways. Use a suitable presser foot so that the needle doesn't break.

Thread take-up lever
This feeds the correct amount of thread from the spool down through to the needle.

Tension-regulating dial
The tension dial alters the tension on the top thread.

Thread-cutter
This is situated at the back of the machine for cutting threads.

Thread-holder pin
This holds the reel of thread when filling the bobbin and stitching.

Threading the upper machine

Unless a machine is threaded in exactly the right sequence it won't work properly. Every machine has a slightly different sequence, but in all of them the thread goes between the tension discs and back up through the take-up lever before it is threaded through the needle.

Always have the take-up lever at its highest point before threading. This brings the needle up to its highest point and lines up all the mechanical parts inside the sewing machine ready for inserting the filled bobbin case. The manual accompanying your sewing machine should have a diagram showing the correct threading sequence for your particular model.

Horizontal thread-holders on the upper machine have a clip to hold the reel in position. The thread unwinds off one end of the stationary reel. Vertical thread-holders have a disc of felt to help the reel to spin around as the machine is working.

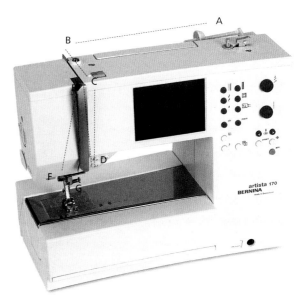

1 Fit the reel on to the thread-holder (A), making sure that the thread can come off freely. Take the thread round B, between the tension disks (C) and down under the first thread guide (D).

2 Put the thread into the top of the take-up lever (E) and then through the thread guides (F) leading down to the needle (G). Thread the needle from the grooved side (front to back).

Filling the bobbin

1 Fill the bobbin using the bobbin-winding mechanism on the machine. To begin, pass the end of the thread through one of the small holes in the side and fit it on to the spindle.

2 Click the bobbin-winding mechanism into place. This should automatically stop the machine from stitching – if not, you will have to loosen the stop motion knob on the hand wheel. The bobbin will fill automatically to the correct level.

3 Insert the bobbin into the bobbin case (A) so that the thread is pulled back on itself through the spring (B).

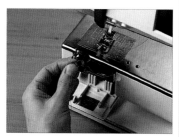

4 Fit the bobbin case into the machine, holding the case by the lever on the back. The open lever locks the bobbin into the case.

5 Push the case into the socket until it clicks, then release the lever. Close the cover. If it does not click, the mechanism inside is not aligned.

The bobbin thread

1 To raise the bobbin thread, thread the needle and hold the upper thread out to one side. Some machines have an automatic thread-lifting mechanism but otherwise turn the hand wheel forwards until the needle has gone down and up again. Pull the upper thread to bring the bobbin thread right out. Take both threads through the slot in the presser foot and out of the back.

Choosing a needle

Always select a machine needle to suit the thread and fabric you are using; this will reduce the likelihood of the needle breaking.

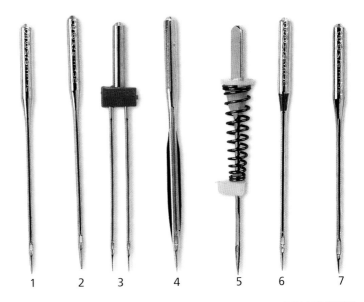

1   2   3   4   5   6   7

1 Universal needles

Universal sewing machine needles range in size from 70/9, used for fine fabrics to 110/18, used for heavy-weight fabrics. Size 80/12 is ideal for medium-weight fabric. Keep a selection to hand and change your needle when using different weights of fabric. A fine needle will break if the fabric is too thick and a large needle will damage a fine fabric.

2 Ballpoint needles

Ballpoint needles are used for synthetic fabrics, jersey and elastic. They have a round end which pushes between the threads instead of piercing them. This type of needle can also be used with fine silks and delicate fabrics which may snag.

3 Twin needles

Twin needles consist of two needles fitted to the one shank. They are used to sew narrow, parallel lines or, when the machine tension is altered, to sew pin tucks. You can also buy special stretch twin needles for working on jersey fabrics. When threading the machine with these needles, you will need two reels of thread. For best results, take one thread down each side of the central tension disc.

4 Wing needles

Wing needles have a wide blade on each side of the shaft, which cuts a decorative groove in the fabric as you stitch.

5 Spring needles

A spring needle allows you to embroider without a darning foot or embroidery hoop because it stops the fabric from moving about.

6 Embroidery needles

Embroidery needles have larger eyes than normal to allow sewing with a wide range of decorative threads. Some special embroidery needles have extremely large eyes for the thicker threads.

7 Top-stitch needles

Top-stitch needles have a very large eye to accommodate a thick, decorative thread.

FITTING THE NEEDLE

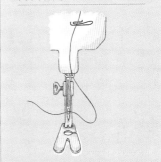

Machine needles can only be fitted one way because they have a flat surface down one side (the shank) and a long groove down the other side (the shaft). When the needle is inserted, this groove should line up directly with the last thread guide. When the machine is in use, the thread runs down the groove and scores a unique channel into the metal. So when you change thread, you should change your needle, too.

Machine feet

All machines have a number of interchangeable feet for different types of sewing. The most common ones are illustrated here but you can buy other specialist feet. These are designed for particular functions such as getting close to a zipper or guiding thread, cord or fabric while sewing.

Clear-view foot

Similar to the general-purpose foot, this foot allows you to see where you are stitching. It can be cut away or made from clear plastic. It can also be used for satin stitch because the underside of the foot is cut away to prevent the stitching from being flattened. Use it when working with bulky fabrics.

Hemming foot

A hemming foot has a curled piece of metal that turns a rolled hem on fine fabrics and feeds it under the needle. The hem can then be stitched with straight or fancy stitches.

Cording foot

This foot has a groove underneath which guides cord, round elastic or narrow ribbon under the needle for stitching.

Blind-hemming (blind-stitching) foot

This foot has a metal guide for a turned-back hem. It is possible to adjust the needle position so that just a few threads are caught when stitching.

General-purpose foot

The basic metal general-purpose foot shown is used for all general straight stitching and zigzag on ordinary fabrics.

Darning foot

A darning foot is used for machine darning and free-style machine embroidery. The feed teeth on the machine are always lowered and the fabric is held flat against the needle plate using an embroidery hoop upside down. Set the stitch length at zero and sew straight stitch or zigzag with this foot.

Zipper foot

This allows you to stitch close to zipper teeth or piping. The needle can be adjusted to sew on either side. A special zipper foot is available to guide the teeth of invisible zippers.

Buttonhole foot

This foot has two grooves underneath to guide rows of satin stitch forwards and backwards, leaving a tiny gap between for cutting.

Spacing guide (seam guide)

This attachment can be used with a variety of different feet as long as the rod and clip fits. By sliding the rod along, a particular distance can be stitched accurately. This guide is useful for stitching curves and for machine quilting.

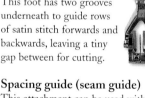

Stitch tension

A new machine will have the tension correctly set, with the dial at the marked centre point. Try out any stitches you intend to use on a sample of your fabric.

To check the tension, bring all the pattern and zigzag dials back to zero and set the stitch length between 2 and 3 for normal stitching. Place a folded strip of fabric on the needle plate, lower the needle into the fabric and sew a row of straight stitches. These should look exactly the same on both sides.

Above: The top and bottom threads lock together correctly in the middle of the fabric when the machine tension is correct.

Above: The top tension is loose and it is pulled to the wrong side of the fabric.

Above: The top thread tension is too tight.

Altering tension

To tighten the tension, turn the dial towards the lower numbers. To loosen it, turn towards the higher numbers. This will automatically affect the tension of the thread coming through the bobbin case. If the top tension dial is far from the centre, the spring on the bobbin case is probably wrong.

Only alter the lower tension as a last resort. You should be able to dangle the bobbin case without the thread slipping through. Shake the thread and the bobbin case should drop a little. Turn the screw on the side of the bobbin case slightly to alter the tension. Try out the stitching again on a sample of fabric and alter the top tension this time until the stitch is perfect.

Maintenance and trouble shooting

Like a car, a sewing machine will only run well if it is used regularly and looked after. It needs to be oiled on a regular basis and cleaned out – this may be several times during the making of curtains or a garment. General maintenance only takes a few minutes but will ensure that your machine works well and lasts longer between services. Cleaning is essential when you change fabrics, especially if it is from a dark to a light-coloured one. Remove the sewing machine needle. Use a stiff brush to clean out the fluff (lint) along the route the top thread takes through the machine. Unscrew the needle plate and brush out any fluff from around the feed teeth. Remove the bobbin case to check that no thread is trapped in the mechanism.

Oil the machine from time to time using your handbook as a guide. Only use a couple of drops – too much oil can be damaging. Leave the machine overnight with a fabric pad beneath the presser foot and then wipe the needle before use. Some new machines are self-lubricating.

Even if you take care of your machine, problems can occur. Some of the more common problems are listed below.

The machine works too slowly
The machine may have two speeds and may be set on slow. More likely, it hasn't been used for a while and oil could be clogging the working parts. Run the machine without a needle for a minute to loosen all the joints. Check that the foot control is not obstructed. As a last resort, ask a dealer to check the tension belt.

No stitches form
Ensure the bobbin is full and inserted correctly. Check that the needle is facing in the right direction and threaded from the grooved side.

Above: Lace and velvet require extreme care when sewing. Always test a sample first to establish the correct tension.

The needle doesn't move
Check that the balance wheel is tight and that the bobbin winder is switched off. If the needle still doesn't move there may be thread trapped in the sewing hook behind the bobbin case. Remove the bobbin case and take hold of the thread end. Rock the balance wheel backwards and forwards until it comes out.

The machine jams
Rock the balance wheel gently to loosen the threads and take the fabric out. Remove the needle, unscrew the needle plate and brush out any fluff. Alternatively check that the machine is correctly threaded and the fabric is far enough under the presser foot when beginning.

The needle bends or breaks
A needle will break if it hits the foot, bobbin case or needle plate on a machine. Check that you are using the correct foot. When using a zipper foot, a common mistake is forgetting to move the needle to the left or right for straight stitching or to zigzag. Check the bobbin case is inserted properly. Make sure the take-up lever is at its highest point before fitting.

A needle that has been bent will break if it hits the needle plate. To avoid bent needles, sew slowly over

pins and thick seams. A needle will also bend if there is a knot in the thread or if the fabric is pulled through the machine faster than the machine is sewing.

Fabric does not feed through
This can happen when the feed teeth are lowered in the darning position. Close zigzag or embroidery stitches will bunch up in the general-purpose foot, so change the foot to one that is cut away underneath to allow the stitches to feed through.

Stitches are different lengths
Check whether the needle is blunt or unsuitable for the fabric and that it is inserted correctly. Try stitching with the needle in the left or right position. On fine fabrics, put tissue paper under the presser foot.

The top thread keeps breaking
Manufacturers recommend that you change needles every time you change the type of thread. This is because each thread type scores a unique channel through the needle groove which will cause a different type of thread to snag and break. Label your needle packet to indicate what type of thread to use with each needle. This is particularly important when doing machine embroidery. Check that you are using the correct thread and type of needle for the fabric. A knot or slub in the thread may also cause the thread to break.

The bobbin thread breaks
Check that the bobbin case is inserted correctly, has not been overfilled and the thread has no knots in it. Also check the bobbin case mechanism for trapped fluff. Occasionally, the spring on the bobbin case is too tight for the thread and the tension screw has to be loosened – refer to your user manual for instructions.

Templates

Enlarge the templates to the desired size, using a photocopier. Alternatively, trace the design and draw a grid of evenly spaced squares over your tracing. Draw a larger grid on to another piece of paper and copy the outline square by square.

Cable pattern

Feathered Heart

Feather/ring design
with lattice pattern

Lover's Knot

Quilting templates,
p.71

Feathered Wheel

Feathered Triangle

Plaited Border

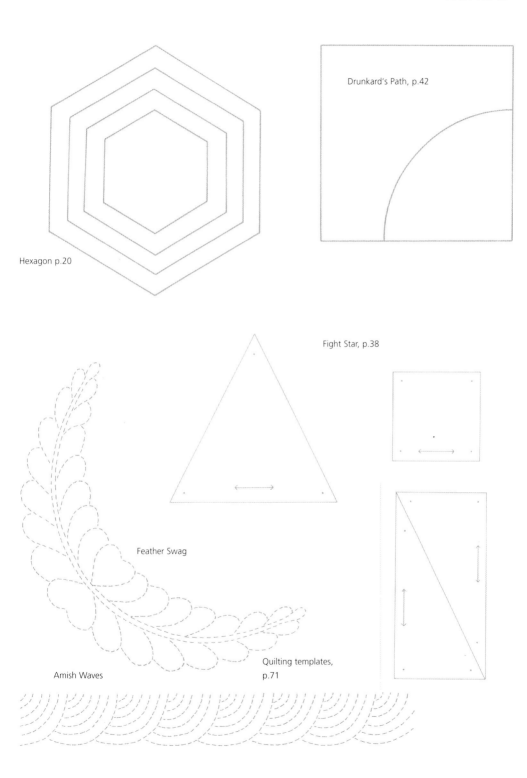

Drunkard's Path, p.42

Hexagon p.20

Fight Star, p.38

Feather Swag

Amish Waves

Quilting templates,
p.71

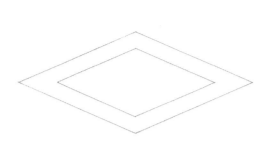

Le Moyne Star and Virginia Star p.40

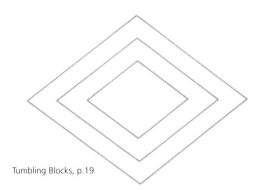

Tumbling Blocks, p.19

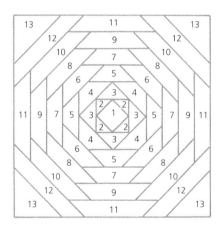

Log Cabin, p.51

Pineapple Log Cabin, p.52

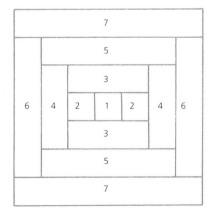

Courthouse Steps, p.53

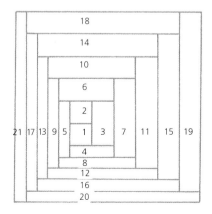

Off-centre Log Cabin, p.53

Stained glass appliqué,
p.64

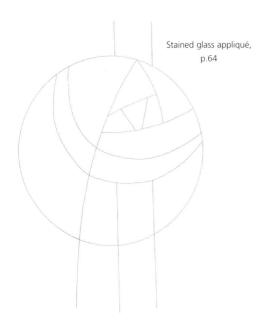

Baltimore quilt, p.60

Reverse appliqué,
p.66

Italian and Trapunto quilting,
p.76–77

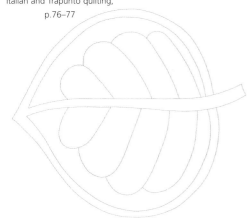

Shadow appliqué,
p.62

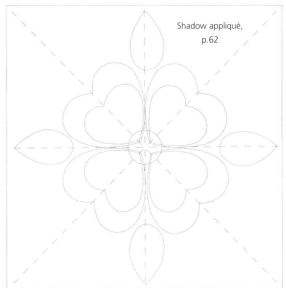

INDEX

SUPPLIERS

United Kingdom
Barnyarns Ltd
PO Box 28
Thirsk
North Yorkshire, YO7 3YN
for sewing and embroidery supplies

Bogod Machine Company
50–52 Great Sutton Street
London, EC1V ODJ
for sewing machines and overlockers

Coats Crafts
McMullen Road
Darlington
Co. Durham, DL1 1YQ
*for machine embroidery and
sewing threads*

Delicate Stitches
339 Kentish Town Road
Kentish Town
London
NW5 2TJ
for fine natural fabrics

DMC Creative World
Pullman Road
Wigston
Leicestershire, LE18 2DY
*for counted-thread fabrics, embroi-
dery thread and crewel wool*

Duttons for Buttons
3 Church Street
Ilkley, LS29 9DR
(branches in Harrogate, Keighley,
York and Leeds)
for buttons

Newey Goodman
Sedgley Road
West Tipton
West Midlands
DY4 8AH
for sewing equipment

Quorn Country Crafts
18 Churchgate
Loughborough
Leicestershire
for patchwork fabrics

France
La Maison du Patchwork
29 rue Jeanne d'Arc
87290 Châteauponsac
France
*for patchwork and quilting holiday
workshops*

United States
Aardvark Adventures
PO Box 2449
Livermore, CA94551
for fabrics, threads and trims

Herrschers
Hoover Road
Stevens Point, WI 54481
for general tools and equipment

Nancy's Notions
PO Box 683
Dept 32, Beave Dam
WI 53916
*for sewing, quilting, beadwork,
appliqué and embroidery*

Canada
Dressew
337 W Hastings Street
Vancouver, BC

Australia
Coats Patons Crafts Pty Ltd
89–91 Peters Avenue
Mulgrave
VIC 3170

DMC Needlecraft Pty Ltd
51–55 Carrington Road
Marrickville
NSW 2204

Simply Stitches
153 Victoria Avenue
Chatswood
NSW 2067

ACKNOWLEDGEMENTS

The publisher would like to thank the talented stitchers who generously loaned their treasured patchwork for inclusion in this publication: Josephine Bardsley, p.43; Constance Cole, p.61 (designs by Patricia Cox); Greta Fitchett, p.57; Katharine Guerrier, p.61; Helen Keenan, p.67; Barbara Laine, p.78 (left); Sheena Norquay, p.74; Jenny Parks, p.21 (top left); Doreen Plumridge, p.11; Kath Poxon, p.33; Rosemary Richards, p.64; Marie Roper, p.59; Lola Sotorres, p.44; Jean Spencer, p.25; Isabel Sunderland, p.38; Jean Syson, p.72; Gisela Thwaites p.37 and p.73; Caroline Wilkinson, p.50 and 79 (bottom right); Judith Wilson, p.65; and Eiko Yamano, p.45 (top).

Many thanks to the following people for stitching the many samples that appear in this publication: Sue Copeman, Barbara Lethbridge, Joyce Mallinson, Brenda Monk, Kath Poxon, Suraiya Kidia Reed, Lynn Simms, Barbara Smith, Adele and Hayley Wainwright, and Rita Whitehorn.

Thanks also to Bogod Machine Company for the loan of the sewing machine.

Thank you to the following for granting permission to reproduce images: p.53 left, reproduced by permission of the American Museum in Britain, Bath ©; p.14, Christies Images Ltd 1999; p.27 Lady of the Lake, Amish quilt, American, c.1930, private collection; p.45, crazy patchwork quilt, c.1875, Smithsonian Institution, Washington DC, USA; p.81 Railroad, American quilt, c.1900, private collection; and p.83 Double Wedding Ring, American quilt, c.1930, private collection, all from The Bridgeman Art Library; and p.18 V&A Picture Library.